Innovation management

イノベーション・マネジメント研究

2012 No.8

contents

論　文	Green Innovation – is it really Green? Michael NORTON …… 1	
	Manufacturing Engineering in Europe and Japan: A Preliminary Comparative Case Study of Two Automotive Component Suppliers Mihail MARINOV, Daniel Arturo HELLER …… 17	
研究ノート	フラッグキャリアの「生産調整」について ―1990年代から2000年代にかけてのBAヨーロッパ路線― 柴田匡平 …… 32	
調査報告	信州大学学生の環境とエネルギーに対する意識についての一考察 並木光行 …… 42	
	イノベーション・マネジメント専攻での教育体験に対する 　修了生の意識調査　結果報告　　今村英明、高相　栄美 …… 50	

Journal of Innovation Management

2012　No.8

Papers

Green Innovation - is it really Green?
　　　　Michael NORTON ··· 1

Manufacturing Engineering in Europe and Japan: A Preliminary Comparative Case
Study of Two Automotive Component Suppliers
　　　　Mihail MARINOV, Daniel Arturo HELLER ·· 17

Production Adjustment in BA's shorthaul operation in the 1990s and 2000s
　　　　Kyohei SHIBATA ··· 32

Survey Reports

Recognitions and Perceptions of Shinshu University Students on Environmental and
Energy Issues: A Preliminary Enquiry
　　　　Mitsuyuki NAMIKI ··· 42

Evaluation of the education programme at the Institute of Innovation Management:
An Inquiry to its Alumni in the First Decade
　　　　Hideaki IMAMURA, Emi TAKASOU ·· 50

Green Innovation – is it really Green?

Professor Michael Norton
Environmental Leader Program
Strategic Energy and Resources Management and Sustainable Solutions (SERMSS)
Tohoku University

1 INTRODUCTION

Green Innovation has become a central tenet of government policies in many countries, as one of the policy tools to try and tackle growing environmental problems, particularly those of global warming and climate change. The Green Innovation concept includes the twin objectives of developing environmentally-friendly technologies, policies, processes and markets which combine both environmental and economic objectives. Green innovation has been seen as part of the "Green Economy", the "Green New Deal", and other concepts which see the possibility of merging the twin objectives of encouraging economic development, while at the same time tackling key environmental issues. One of the main targets of Green Innovation is of course the energy system, since this is responsible for a substantial proportion of the greenhouse gas (GHG) emissions of both developed and developing economies, and the term encompasses both technological innovation (for instance more efficient solar panels, new technologies for capturing energy from the sea) and also policy innovations which support the market deployment of renewable energy technologies to replace fossil fuels.

'Green' has however become something of an overused label (as well as its partner label 'eco') in recent years, with the result that its widespread use in the marketing sector has led to skepticism about the credibility of such labels. There are many instances where claims of environmental friendliness have been proved to be misleading; leading to the term "green-washing"[1] to describe situations where the appearance of environmental friendliness or specific sustainability characteristics is not actually based on any real contribution to these attributes. Gillespie (2008) points out that in many cases, the "*greening of the marketplace is little more than a hastily applied veneer of dubious substance*" and that by undermining consumer trust in environmentally friendly products, threatens to undermine the virtuous circle whereby companies producing green products and customers actively selecting them, provides a key driving force towards a more sustainable economy. Japan has seen 'eco' develop as a marketing tool along with 'green' and experienced its own 'green-washing' scandals[2].

With the current focus on Green Innovation, it is important to consider whether similar dangers or weaknesses may occur in the innovation field. To what extent is a 'green' innovation contributing to solving

---

(1) Green-washing is where green PR or green marketing is deceptively used to promote the perception that an organization's aims and products are environmentally friendly. In an annual survey of 'green-washing', one organization examined 5,296 home and family consumer products in North America which made a total of 12,061 green claims. Over 95% of these 'greener' products were found to use some degree of misleading, incomplete or deceitful claims (Futerra, 2011).

(2) For instance in 2008, 17 of the 38 member companies of the Japan Paper Association admitted that they falsified the amounts of recycled paper which had been used in their products. http://www.japantimes.co.jp/text/nb20080119a1.html

current environmental problems, and to what extent is it just a fashionable label to reflect the political priorities of the times? One of the most substantial areas of Green Innovation is currently in the renewable energy field, where initiatives are under way around the world to reduce dependence on fossil fuels. We thus selected as an area for research into the credibility of a Green Innovation, the development of an enhanced renewable energy policy for Japan which followed the Fukushima disaster in 2011. This introduced a Feed-in-Tariff (FIT) system to encourage renewable sources of energy, which currently include solar, wind, geothermal and biomass. This paper looks at the potential implications for the environment and other sustainability issues of the policy developed for biomass energy, and how the policy process did or did not give adequate consideration to the environmental and sustainability ('green') implications of policy. We find that in this case, the use of policy innovation (through the FIT system) to encourage technological innovation in biomass energy, failed to ensure that the developments were in fact 'green'.

2 BACKGROUND

2.1 JAPAN'S GREEN INNOVATION POLICY

Japan has developed over several years, a series of policies to encourage technological innovation in the resource and energy fields. Approaches include (Norton, 2010):

- A legal framework aimed at a 'resource-cycling' and 'energy-efficient' Society[3].
- Various government-funded initiatives such as Eco-towns, Top Runner[4].
- R&D programs on renewable energy technologies through the New Energy and Industrial Development Organization (NEDO).
- Incentives for low-emission vehicles and efficient electrical appliances which have included an 'eco-points' system, purchasing grants, and vehicle tax reductions.

Through such measures, Japan now offers world-leading 'green' technologies in automotive, electrical goods, solar energy, batteries and other fields. These polices laid the groundwork for a more focused priority on Green Innovation in the last 5 years. First to draw attention to the importance of Green Innovation was the "Innovation 25" initiative (Cabinet Office, 2007) which pointed out that without control of global warming and reducing the over-use of natural resources, the global environment and economy will be unable to sustain current consumption patterns and may collapse. "Innovation 25" recommended that sustainability be a key national objective, and that Japan should build on its strengths in resource and energy efficiency, to develop more sustainable technologies and businesses. Similar thinking was found in the "Plan for a Leading Environmental Nation" which emphasized that global environmental problems pose a serious challenge to humanity's well-being (Cabinet Office, 2007a). Such visions see a 'win-win' situation whereby innovation towards an energy and resource-efficient economy will strengthen both Japanese competitiveness and contribute to regional sustainability.

Green Innovation also emerged as one of two priority areas for Japan's publicly-funded R&D in the 4th Basic Science and Technology Plan. As explained in the plan document (Cabinet Office 2010), the promotion of "Green Innovation" would "*aim to solve the climate change issues facing Japan and the world... realize the world's most advanced low-carbon society by identifying trends in de-fossil fuel that many countries are developing competitively as a key to future growth. Such promotion is expected to facilitate further innovation of environmental /energy technologies, in which Japan has strengths, and promote the reform of social systems and institutions. With such prevalence and development of Green Innovation at home and abroad, Japan will achieve sustainable growth.*"

---

(3) These include the Basic Law for establishing a Material-cycling Society, the Green Purchasing Law, the Waste Management Law, the Law for Promotion of Effective Utilization of Resources, the Container and Packaging Recycle Law, the Home Appliance Recycle Law, the Vehicle Recycle Law, the Construction Material Recycle Law, and the Food Recycle Law.

(4) The Top Runner policy is aimed at continuous improvement of energy efficiency in designated categories of electrical appliances and administered by the Energy Conservation Centre.

FIGURE 1　JAPAN'S ELECTRICITY GENERATION BY ENERGY SOURCE TO 2010

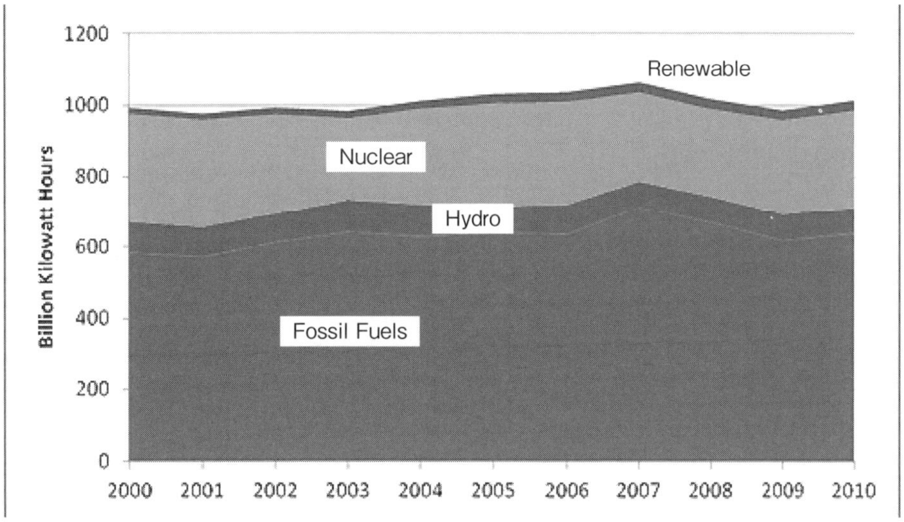

Most recently, Green Innovation has been included in the "Japan Rebirth Strategy" following the 2011 earthquake and tsunami. This recognizes that Japan faces several challenges, including reconstructing areas affected by the earthquake, tsunami and nuclear accident, at the same time as addressing socio-demographic (ageing society) and economic challenges, as well as reviewing its energy mix. As a result, four policy areas are assigned priority in government policy: "green", "life", "agriculture", and "small and medium enterprises" (NPU, 2012). Green Innovation is thus clearly established as a priority for R&D, environment and economic policy. Let us first consider the current environmental situation before considering the role of biomass in renewable energy.

2.2 Japan's GHG reduction targets and trends

Japan's GHG emissions were 1.26 billion metric tons (bmt) in the Kyoto baseline year of 1990. While they had grown to near 1.4bmt by 2007, the economic decline after the 2008 financial shock reduced emissions to 1.206bmt in 2009, while they recovered to 1.258bmt in 2010. With regard to future targets on GHG emissions, the then LDP Government announced in mid-2009 that it would adopt a target for 2020 of a 15% reduction in emissions based on 2005, amounting to an 8% reduction on the Kyoto baseline of 1990. The new Democratic Party-led coalition government of 2009 made an early announcement that it would adopt a target for 2020 of a net reduction of 25% relative to 1990. Both governments had agreed with the longer term G8 target of a reduction in emissions by 80% by 2050.

Energy use for electricity generation is the largest single source of GHG emissions and until 2011 relied on thermal power stations for ～60%, hydro for ～4% and nuclear for ～30% of electricity generated. Renewables accounted for ～2% in 2010 (Figure 1). Japan's 54 nuclear reactors produced 274 TWh of electricity in 2010, and policy was then to increase nuclear's share of total electricity generation from 24 percent in 2008 to 40 percent by 2017, and to 50 percent by 2030. Nuclear thus provided a critical tool for meeting the country's targets for GHG reduction.

After the 2011 Great Eastern Japan Earthquake and Tsunami, the resulting disaster at the Fukushima Daichi power station, led to the sequential closure of all Japan's nuclear power reactors, since local and national opposition and new safety regulations made it extremely difficult to restart reactors temporarily shutdown for routine maintenance. At the time of writing (January 2013) only 2 of the 54 had been restarted, leading to a substantial increase in the use of fossil fuels with adverse effects on both GHG emissions and the trade balance. The Ministry of the Environment announced in December 2012 that GHG emissions for the year April 2010 to March 2011 rose to 13.7bmt- a 3.9% increase on 2010, primarily due to the switch from nuclear to fossil fuels (MOE, 2012).

FIGURE 2   SHIFTS TO A SUSTAINABILITY-ORIENTED INNOVATION SYSTEM IN 2012

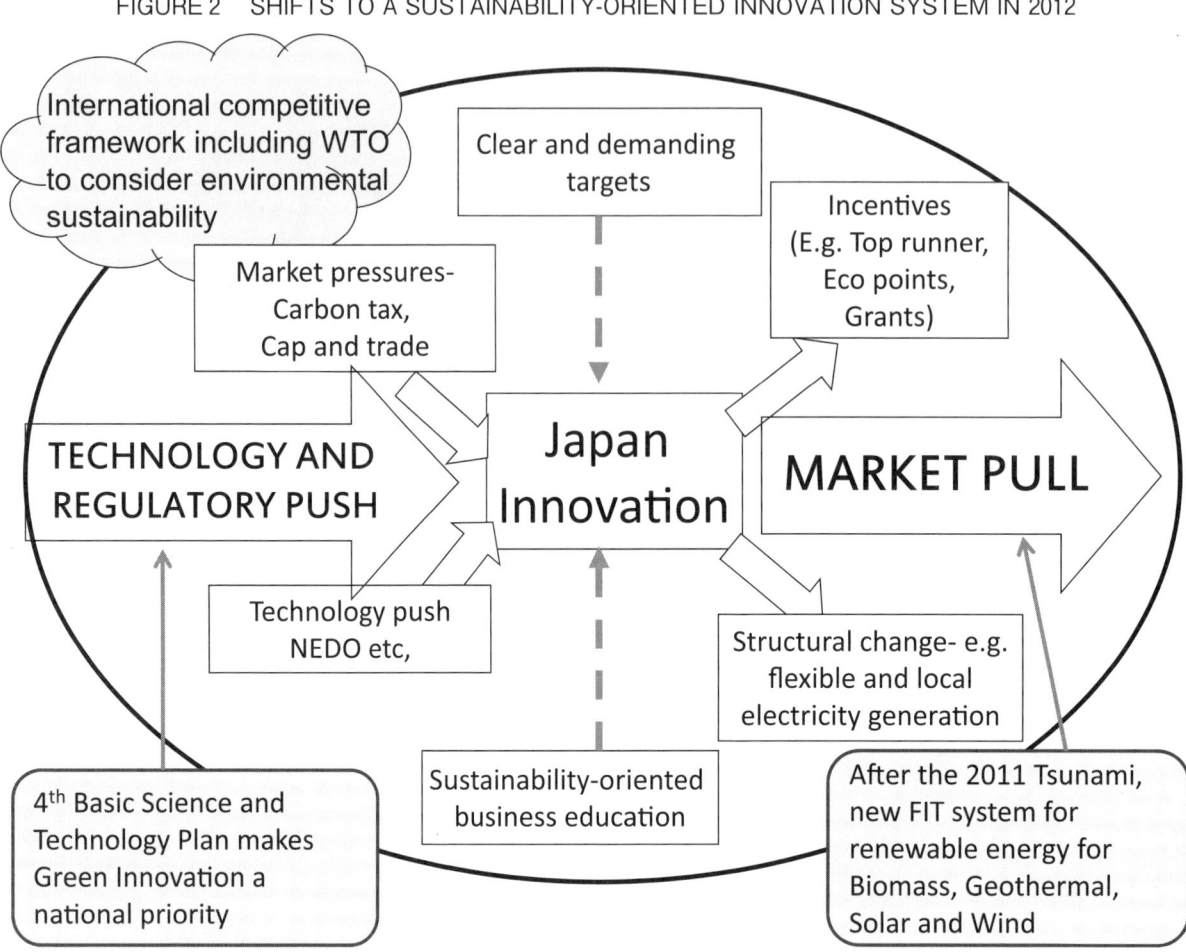

2.3 Policies following the 2011 Great Eastern Japan Earthquake and Tsunami

In response to increased public concerns over continued reliance on nuclear power, the Government announced in July 2011 a new policy to promote renewable energies; with particular focus on solar, wind, geothermal and biomass. Instead of the anticipated increase in nuclear capacity before the disaster, the new policy shifts the priority to renewable sources. The target is to obtain 13% of energy from renewable sources by 2013, 20% by 2020, and a long-term goal of 25-35% by 2030 (Prime Minister's Office, 2011). The key policy measure to achieve these targets is a Feed-in-Tariff (FIT) system whereby utilities are obliged to pay nationally-decided rates to suppliers of electricity from photovoltaic, wind, geothermal and biomass sources.

As pointed out earlier (Norton, 2010, 2012), this range of measures can be seen as components of a **Sustainability-oriented Innovation System,** which recognizes that technological innovations need to be supported by regulatory and market pull measures to be successful. Systematic innovation towards an energy and resource efficient Japan may require a framework containing (Norton, 2010):

- Technology push through existing programmes of technology development aimed at specific targets such as improved efficiencies in solar energy.
- Supportive market incentives (market pull)- grants for solar panels, subsidies for environmentally friendly vehicles, etc.
- Market push: shift economic signals towards improved resource and energy efficiency by a shift to environmentally-based taxes, cap and trade systems or both.
- Infrastructure to encourage a low carbon infrastructure – e.g. smart grid to make it easier for dispersed renewable supplies to feed into the grid.
- Encourage international trade to place a higher priority on the sustainability of products and production processes.

The new policy on renewable energy can be seen as

a strengthening of this innovation system as shown in Figure 2. The FIT system is a critical mechanism of 'market pull', while the emphasis on Green Innovation in the 4th Basic Plan for Science and Technology comprises a strengthening in the 'technology push' part of the system.

With the increased focus on renewable energy increasing support for biomass, let us now consider the environmental implications.

3 BIOMASS AS RENEWABLE ENERGY AND ENVIRONMENTAL IMPLICATIONS

Energy from biomass first emerged on a large scale as liquid biofuels in the 1970s, when the aim was to strengthen national energy self-sufficiency by replacing gasoline from oil, with fuels such as ethanol and biodiesel produced from sugar or other domestically cultivated crops. Since concerns over global warming grew, biofuels have become one of the 'renewable' energies which can contribute to greenhouse gas reduction strategies. With the substantial increase in liquid biofuels in recent years, concerns have already been raised over the effects of competition between biofuel crops and food crops, and on demands for additional land for their production (Royal Society, 2008; Nuffield Council on Bioethics, 2011; EU, 2011; Bergsma et al, 2010). In recent years, solid biomass for heat and/or electricity generation has attracted attention and large scale co-firing of wood chips in coal-fired power stations has been reported in Europe and Japan (EU, 2010).

Biomass is regarded as 'renewable' energy and included in a number of countries' strategies to reduce GHG emissions because it is assumed to be 'carbon neutral'. This is because the carbon in the biomass originated from CO_2 in the atmosphere, absorbed by leaves and converted by photosynthesis to woody material. The CO_2 emitted when the biomass is burnt is thus returning CO_2 already absorbed, and it is assumed that the carbon released will be re-absorbed when the trees or other biomass crops regrow. For this reason, emissions from biomass are not currently accounted for in the energy sector when countries report under the UN Framework Convention on Climate Change (UNFCCC); instead biomass-related emissions are meant to be measured and reported under the 'land use, land use change and forestry' (LULUCF) category, which many nations do not report. This means biofuels can be used in transport, or solid biomass in power stations with the appearance that no carbon has been released from their combustion! In the electricity sector, a country can thus import biomass as a substitute for coal, and ignore the GHG emissions at the combustion stage, so that it can claim that its CO_2 emissions per unit of electricity generated have been reduced. In fact, the amounts of CO_2 emitted from the stack are not reduced, but this 'accounting trick' has already been used in Japan by electricity generators using imported biomass to co-fire in coal-fired powers stations, in order to "*reduce the carbon intensity of electricity generation*" (Keidanren, 2009). Such accounting distortions may be insignificant if biomass does, in reality, reduce overall carbon dioxide atmospheric concentrations, so let us consider whether this is so.

Issues relevant to Japan's biomass policy can be assessed from an analysis of European experience. Liquid biofuels are already regulated under the Renewable Energy Directive (RED) which sets minimum standards for reducing GHG emissions across the complete life cycle (from biomass production to final production of energy), and seeks to avoid damaging effects on biodiversity where biomass is taken from sources such as forests without regard to sustainability and legality[5].

With solid biomass used for electricity, heating or cooling (EU, 2010), setting detailed rules is the responsibility of Member States, but the main sustainability issues are in Table 1.

---

(5) The RED (EU, 2008) specifies:
- Minimum of 35% GHG saving compared to fossil fuel (rising to 50% in 2017, and 60% in 2018 for new installations);
- General restrictions on using biomass materials sourced from land with high biodiversity value or high carbon stock – including primary forest, peatland and wetlands.

TABLE 1 SUSTAINABILITY ISSUES FOR SOLID BIOMASS

Issue	Comment
Land management, cultivation and harvesting of biomass	Sustainability concerns include how to protect forest ecosystems and carbon stocks. In particular, whether increased demand for biomass feedstock will impact carbon stocks in forests and agricultural land and soils, and damage biodiversity.
Land use, land use change and forestry accounting	Deforestation, forest degradation and other practices can result in a significant loss of terrestrial carbon and/or significant changes in productivity. Emissions related to land use, land use change and forestry (LULUCF) thus need to be properly accounted for.
Life cycle greenhouse gas performance	Life Cycle Assessment (LCA) shows that the GHG balance of bio-energy systems depends on the type of feedstock, carbon stock changes due to land use change, transport, feedstock processing method, and what methods are used to produce heat or electricity.
Energy conversion efficiency	This is critical to overall GHG reduction performance, so support schemes need to differentiate in favour of installations that achieve high energy conversion efficiencies, such as cogeneration plants.

Source: adapted from EU (2010).

In the EU, it is expected that solid biomass should be subject to similar restrictions on efficiency and sources to those for liquid biomass already mentioned under the RED. However, when biomass is sourced from forests, additional issues arise with respect to the source of wood and the sustainability of the forest management involved. The UK is one of the first Member States to act on the sustainability of solid biomass used for energy generation and has set criteria as (DECC 2011, 2011a):

  - Minimum of 60% GHG lifecycle emission saving for electricity generation across the life cycle (relative to fossil fuel);
  - Restrictions on using biomass sourced from land with high biodiversity value or high carbon stock –including from primary forest, peatlands and wetlands;
  - Information reporting is required on biomass type, format, mass or volume, country of origin, whether waste, energy crop or by-product, if it meets an environmental standard and the name of the standard, plus details of land use changes since January 2008;
  - When the biomass used is virgin wood, this should be sourced from a sustainably managed forest, whether domestic or imported.

There are also scientific issues which have emerged since the RED regulations were adopted, which raise additional questions over the environmental impact of biomass. There are three main issues:

Carbon neutrality and carbon debt. As already noted, biomass energy is treated as a 'renewable' energy contributing to GHG reductions. In reality however, when forest biomass is burnt, the carbon in the wood is released into the atmosphere immediately. Moreover, as efficiencies of biomass electricity generation may be lower than for fossil fuels, energy from woody biomass can have net GHG emissions per unit of energy that are initially *higher* than those from fossil fuels. It is currently assumed that such emissions are offset through increased absorption of carbon through plant regrowth; but is this the case?

The rates at which the initial carbon release (termed the 'carbon debt') is re-absorbed have been studied for a number of forest-related scenarios (see for example the review by Blomqvist, 2010; Bird et al., 2010 and Hudiberg et al., 2011). Such research indicates that it may take decades or even centuries for carbon released by burning biomass to be re-absorbed. Carbon neutrality is thus a slow process and there are scenarios where such neutrality is never achieved. Using woody biomass for bioenergy is thus **not automatically carbon neutral** (European Environment Agency, 2011). For example the additional CO_2 emissions from a rotation forest in Austria take 280 years to reabsorb (Zanchi et al., 2010). The risks of such long-term carbon debt occurring vary with the source of forest biomass, as summarised in Table 2.

TABLE 2 Carbon debt risk for SOME biomass sources

BIOMASS SOURCE	RISK OF CARBON DEBT
Additional felling in managed forests	High
Extraction of harvest residues from managed forests	Low
Reinstating management in neglected woodlands: clearfelling	High
Reinstating management in neglected woodlands: thinning	Medium
Felling of old-growth forests	High
New forest plantations replacing permanent grassland	Low
New forest plantations replacing mature forest	High

Source: adapted from Blomqvist (2010).

The fact that biomass energy may lead to an initial increase in GHG emissions, and may only reduce them over a long period, has implications for climate change policy. The scientific advice on avoiding dangerous climate change, is that global emissions of GHG must start to decline within the next few years and halve by 2050 (IPCC, 2007). By releasing as much (if not more) GHG than fossil fuels in the short term, biomass energy makes no contribution to short-term climate change strategy. Whether biomass can contribute over the critical 20-40 year time scale depends on the source of the biomass and its regrowth rate. As a consequence, there is a scientific argument that biomass should only be classified as a renewable energy contributing to climate change policies, when it produces a GHG saving over a climate-relevant timescale (10-40 years). Energy from waste and currently unused residues could meet this condition, but biomass derived from felling forests may not.

Carbon accounting. This second issue relates to the current guidance that emissions from bioenergy should be accounted for under the category of LULUCF (Table 1), and not when the biomass is burnt. Reporting LULUCF emissions is voluntary; many countries do not report, and thus many of the emissions from burning forest biomass are ignored.[6]

Indirect Land Use Change. This third issue arises because land allocated to biomass production is no longer available for the previous use (e.g. crops for food or animal feed). The previous demand is thus shifted to new areas, leading to additional deforestation or land conversion with associated impacts on GHG emissions, biodiversity and the people dependent on the land converted (IEEP, 2010). One analysis (Bergsma et al., 2010) suggests that meeting current targets in the EU for biofuels by 2020 will lead to the conversion of 69,000 km^2 of land across the world to compensate for the areas dedicated to biofuels- just to supply EU demand (for oil seeds, palm oil, sugar cane, wheat, etc.). The European Environment Agency scientific committee has concluded (European Environment Agency, 2011) that ILUC is potentially a very significant factor, and has the potential to release enough GHG to negate the savings from conventional biofuels. Such factors may also apply were land to be switched from agricultural use to plantation forests for solid biomass. In view of the historical impact of Japan's imports of timber[7] on the forests of other countries, there are grounds for concern over the potential environmental impact of increasing imports of biomass. A FIT system which led to large scale imports of biomass without appropriate criteria on the sustainability of supplies could thus accelerate deforestation in supplier countries, contributing to biodiversity loss

---

(6) Negotiations are underway in the appropriate international fora to resolve this anomaly, and national policies which exploit current rules to create the appearance of GHG reductions would be exposed as meaningless and counter-productive were the rules to be changed.

and increased carbon emissions.

With the existing precedent of standards on liquid biomass (both on GHG minimum reduction requirements and in protecting the environment and biodiversity at the biomass source), and the serious scientific questions over the environmental impact of solid biomass, the new FIT system introduced in 2011 faces a number of challenges to ensure its 'greenness'. To evaluate its performance against these challenges, we first need to establish relevant sustainability criteria. For this, we set up a project to develop a consensus among key stakeholders of the sustainability criteria which should be applied to solid biomass in the FIT system. This project started in July 2011 and was completed in June 2012.[8]

4 DEVELOPING A CONSENSUS ON SUSTAINABILITY CRITERIA

Stakeholders with a link to biomass energy include those involved in the regulatory process. Government departments with relevant responsibilities include the Forest Agency (FA) of the Ministry of Agriculture Forestry and Fisheries (MAFF) which is concerned with the economic value of local forests. Both FA and Ministry of the Environment (MOE) are concerned with illegal logging, while the Ministry of Economy Trade and Industry (METI) is responsible for the renewable energy system, and the Cabinet Office's National Policy Unit (NPU) for the "National Growth Strategy", in which both renewable energy and local forestry would be promoted.

Japanese departmental structures are characterized by vertical segregation, and previous events have illustrated the tendency for *tatewari gyosei* (vertical administration) where agencies do not always cooperate with each other (e.g. Fukushima, 1995; Amyx, 2004). METI's priority is economic development and it has no direct remit for sustainability. Furthermore, even the MOE and FA do not have a strong position on sustainability of timber, because as already noted (footnote 7), the current rules on green purchasing focus on legality and not sustainability.

Turning to stakeholders outside government, a number of non-governmental organizations (NGOs) have been concerned with renewable energy in general, biomass in particular, and issues of environmental sustainability (Table 3).

The above stakeholders (both government and non-government) were invited to join a stakeholder engagement process, whose purpose would be to consider the main issues of:

a) Environmental impacts: in particular the net reduction in CO_2 emissions resulting from the use of solid biomass over the full lifecycle.

b) Biomass feedstock sustainability. This includes the criteria for assessing the impact on sustainability in the source country, certification systems, and ILUC issues.

c) Energy security: one objective of renewable energy policy is to strengthen Japan's energy security, raising the issue of how to approach imports and domestic sources.

d) Economic aspects; biomass has the potential to help revitalise Japanese forestry and local economies by creating a new market for forestry residues and/or biomass-oriented forestry. On the other hand it has the potential to distort current markets if it creates demand for sources of timber currently used in lumber, paper or board.

All the NGOs and some government departments were willing to participate in the consensus process, but two key government departments declined to do so. This meant that the original target of developing a consensus between the regulators and the external stakeholders had to be modified. Instead it was decided to first develop a consensus among the external stake-

---

(7) Japan, despite 2/3 of it area being forest, relies extensively on imports for timber. Such imports have exerted major impacts on supplier countries' forests and their environment, and supplies have shifted as forest resources in one country after another have been depleted. Until 2006, there were no requirements in either the private or public sectors in Japan related to legality or sustainability of timber imports, but the Green Purchasing Law was amended in April 2006 to limit government procurement of wood and wood products to those with verified legality (Ministry of the Environment, 2007).

(8) The project was supported by the British Embassy's Prosperity Fund.

TABLE 3   NGO STAKEHOLDERS

Organization	Main Interests
The Biomass Industrial Society Network	Promoting use of biomass from economic, social, and environmental sustainability viewpoints.
Institute for Sustainable Energy Policies	Reforming energy policy, including both abolishing nuclear and promoting renewable energy sources.
The Pellet Club	Promoting wood pellets market in Japan, by networking citizens and local government, and the industrial sector.
WWF Japan, FoE Japan, and Global Environmental Forum	Promoting sustainable forest management and combating illegal logging to promote sustainable development especially in the developing world.
Japan for Sustainability	Providing information on developments and activities in Japan that lead toward sustainability.

holders and subsequently use that consensus to influence the policy process. The consensus development process used stakeholder roundtable meetings at which the key issues above were addressed. The process and its outcome are reported by Norton and Aikawa (2012).

The roundtable meetings revealed some differences between the environmental and industry stakeholders; there was concern that sustainability criteria for biomass could impede future market growth if too burdensome. On the other hand, all stakeholders recognized the potential impacts of Japan's FIT policy on other countries; and also recognized the importance of ensuring that biomass energy did make a real contribution to global warming policy. The stakeholder group succeeded in agreeing a set of core principles and minimum standards necessary for a sustainable FIT system. The final statement agreed by all stakeholders emphasized 3 fundamental principles:

Principle 1: Biomass use should make a real contribution to greenhouse gas (GHG) reductions.
Principle 2: Biomass use should preserve the health of ecosystems.
Principle 3: Biomass use should pay due attention to economic and societal aspects.

The Consensus Statement (see Annex) was issued in January 2012, and circulated to the departments which had been consulted at the first phase of the project. A public symposium was also held (19 March, 2012) which broadened the involvement of other groups and organizations in the debate process.

5 GOVERNMENT PROCESS IN DEVELOPING THE FIT SYSTEM

The 2011 "Renewable Energy Special Measures Law (FIT System)" law required METI to decide the purchasing prices under the new FIT system, taking into consideration the views of other related Ministers (MAFF and MOE included). A *chotatsu kakaku iinkai* (purchasing price expert committee) was established to advise the METI Minister, and the Committee's recommendations were announced on 27 April and set prices for electricity generated by solid biomass in 4 categories[9] (METI, 2012). However, the Committee failed to address sustainability as an issue despite having been informed of the Consensus Statement.

The Stakeholder group members thus submitted additional comments during the public consultation period. These comments pointed out that the Committee had completely ignored the key issue of sustainability, and re-emphasized that:

● Biomass, in contrast with other forms of renewable energy, has many different production

---

(9) These are: unused wood (for example forest residues and thinning) 32 yen; general timber (this would be the category applied to imported wood and chips) 24yen; agricultural and food wastes, and sewage sludge 17yen and recycled wood (from construction demolition etc.) 13yen/KWh.

methods and patterns of supply, with large variations in their potential for reducing GHG emissions and in their effects on ecosystems in the source country.
- For imports it is necessary to consider the potential adverse impacts on the environment and ecosystem in the supplying country.
- Recognizing these special characteristics, internationally, sustainability-related criteria are being applied for both liquid and solid biomass. Moreover, even in Japan standards for sustainability had already been established for liquid biomass, and previously the committee established to look at the basic principles for a FIT system (METI, 2011) had emphasized that:
    1. Biomass should not lead to change from previous uses, or lead to increased prices of previous use products (food supplies, etc.).
    2. Use should be sustainable (should not cause adverse effects on ecosystems or stimulate forest destruction).
    3. Life-cycle assessment should be used to assess the contribution to global warming policy.

METI announced its decision on the FIT for biomass on June 19 (METI, 2012a), and confirmed the Committee recommendations with no significant change. The criteria for solid biomass thus fail to even apply the standards on GHG reductions and protection of biodiversity already adopted in Japan for liquid biofuels.

Norton and Aikawa (2012) examine in more detail the possible reasons for this decision, and METI's responses to points emphasized in the Consensus Statement. The degree of METI's rejection of environmental concerns can be judged from the observation that there is no mention anywhere in the METI response (METI, 2012b) of 'global warming', 'climate change', 'greenhouse gases', 'biodiversity', 'areas of high carbon stock', 'deforestation', 'ILUC', 'LULULF' which are all keywords in the current EU debate on biomass policy, and which were all emphasized in the Consensus Statement. The current FIT system thus fails to evaluate whether or not CO_2 emissions are reduced (even in the long term), or whether harvesting at the biomass source causes adverse environmental impacts or loss of biodiversity.

This rejection of environmental and sustainability considerations, and the treatment of the FIT policy as basically just an economic decision, raises the question whether METI even saw the FIT system as a 'green' innovation issue at all. However, the original Law (Article 1) includes a statement on the Law's purpose which refers to renewables as being important for a stable energy supply and reducing environmental burdens. METI thus had a sufficient mandate to incorporate sustainability criteria. Moreover, the committee established by METI earlier to advise on the framework for the FIT system had already specifically recommended that biomass include criteria on both GHG emission reductions and on the sustainability of the source (METI, 2011).

6 DISCUSSION

This case study suggests that Green Innovation or 'green-motivated' policies need care and support within the overall system if they are to avoid being diverted from their original green target during the implementation phase. In this case, while the initial Government policy had a green objective, this was implicit rather than explicit and thus could be avoided by a combination of an economically focused and 'ungreen' METI, and insufficient commitment by other departments on 'green' issues. Ironically, the METI decision was announced just 1 day before the start of the June 20—22 (2012) 'Rio + 20' conference on sustainable development, and serves to underline the continued challenge of incorporating sustainability considerations into economic and energy policies.

Since the application of the new FIT system, doubts have started to be expressed[10] about the basis for the recommendations of the purchasing price committee, and a new Biomass Industry Association has been established. This will establish a committee to develop a solid biomass use roadmap, and also reconsider the FIT system conditions. This is currently focused

---

(10) See articles at http://wedge.ismedia.jp/articles/-/2371; and http://www.nikkan.co.jp/dennavi/news/nkx0920120710qtkf.html

on economic aspects (especially the pricing formula), but a review process will also provide an opportunity to revisit sustainability issues. It is thus relevant to consider the potential relationship between the economic aspects and potential sustainability criteria. In particular, whether such criteria would benefit or hinder the economic and local revitalization objectives of the biomass policy.

At present, there is no obligation on importers, or local producers to consider sustainability and only a self-regulated obligation to ensure legality. The criteria under sustainability certification schemes (FSC globally, SGEC in Japan[11]) applied to timber and pulp offer one approach to ensuring sustainability, but have been criticized as too complex and expensive to be applied to low-value uses such as biomass. The UK has proposed a median-level approach to create a system which ensures sustainability, while still being practical from the viewpoint of smaller operators who are not registered within internationally-recognized schemes. This 'Category B' approach recognizes that a primary objective of biomass energy is that it be a viable use for currently un-utilized resources such as harvesting residues and small woodland sources. It is thus important that the sustainability criteria be applied without presenting a significant economic or administrative barrier. Equally, because of the danger of large-scale biomass causing serious impacts on the environment, biodiversity and on land rights, such sustainability criteria need to guard against these dangers, especially in imports of wood chips and virgin timber for biomass use.

Where sources or the processing site are already certified under FSC or similar schemes, then proof of source which confirms the certification status (and independent validation) should suffice. However, where such certification is not available, the 'Category B' approach applies a risk assessment approach and offers a flexible alternative which could also be applied in Japan (CPET, 2010). This risk assessment process evaluates the available information on the source to judge whether it is likely that the biomass comes from illegal or poorly regulated sources and adjusts the burden of proof of sustainability required to the risk.

For instance, on legality, the burden of proof for countries with well-established laws and regulations which are competently applied could be met with a standard statement on applicable laws and forestry management processes. On the other hand, for 'high risk' sources or where the source is unknown, proof of compliance **and** independent validation of documentation (to guard against fraud) would be required. The Global Forest Trade Network has lists of applicable laws and required documentation for major countries which would allow such a risk assessment, and is developing a forest legality risk assessment tool. For Japanese timber, the national laws and forestry system are well-developed and all sources could be subject to a 'standard compliance' statement listing applicable laws and forestry planning and management processes. The Forestry Agency could develop a pro-forma to create a standard for Japanese producers to apply.

On sustainability criteria, Japanese compliance with 'Category B' for sources not already certified by FSC or SGEC, would require information based on standard national practice and background information on National, Prefecture and local plans and approvals and how these meet sustainability criteria. This would be similar for most Japanese users and also could be made simpler still by a Forestry Agency pro-forma. Importers would have to provide evidence of the origin and sustainability of the biomass source, together with case-specific data and validation on the source's sustainability when originating from countries where sustainability certification is lacking.

By applying such a flexible risk-assessment based approach, sustainability criteria can be applied equally to biomass inside and outside Japan (as required for WTO compliance), but can be met by a simple 'pro-forma' approach for most local Japanese sources. High risk sources requiring more detailed information and evidence together with independent validations, can be justified under the general duty of 'due diligence'. By avoiding competition from imports which are environmentally damaging, sustainability criteria can create synergy with the primary economic objectives of the FIT process and avoid adding to environmentally destructive practices elsewhere. By assigning a

---

(11) FSC; Forest Stewardship Council. SGEC: Sustainable Green Ecosystem Council.

higher priority to the green aspects, METI could not only protect the green aspects of the FIT biomass policy, but there could even be a potential synergy between the competitive position of Japan-sourced biomass and the sustainability aspects.

（2012年12月21日投稿、2013年1月22日受理）

REFERENCES

Bergsma,G., Croezen, H., Otten, M. and van Valkengoed, M., 2010. Biofuels: indirect land use change and climate impact.
http://www.ce.nl/?go=home.downloadPub&id=1068&file=8169_defreportHCMV.pdf.

Bird, N., Pena, N. and Zanchi., 2010. The upfront carbon debt of bioenergy. http://www.birdlife.org/eu/pdfs/Bioenergy_Joanneum_Research.pdf.

Blomqvist, L., 2010. Understanding the carbon benefits of using woody biomass for bioenergy: unpicking the latest analysis. Report to the Royal Society for the Protection of Birds, UK.

Cabinet Office, 2007. Innovation 25- Creating the Future.
http://www.kantei.go.jp/foreign/innovation/executivesummary.pdf.

Cabinet Office, 2007a. Plan for a Leading Environmental Nation.
http://www.env.go.jp/en/focus/attach/070606-b.pdf

Cabinet Office, 2010. Japan's Science and Technology Basic Policy Report.
http://www8.cao.go.jp/cstp/english/basic/4th-BasicPolicy.pdf#search='basic+science+and+technology+plan'

CPET, 2010. Category B guidance for sustainability of timber. http://www.cpet.org.uk/files/CPET%20Category%20B%20Framework%20July%202010.pdf.

CPET, 2011. UK Government Timber Procurement Policy: Definition of Legal and Sustainable. http://www.cpet.org.uk/files/Definition%20of%20legal%20and%20sustainable%20fourth%20edition%20April%202010.pdf.

DECC, 2011. New Sustainability standards for biomass.
http://www.decc.gov.uk/en/content/cms/meeting_energy/bio_energy/sustainability/sustainability.aspx.

DECC, 2011a. Statutory Consultation on the Renewables Obligation Order 2011. http://www.decc.gov.uk/assets/decc/Consultations/Renewables%20Obligation/261-statutory-con-renewables-obligation.pdf.

EU, 2005. Biomass Action Plan. COM（2005）628 final.

EU, 2008. Directive on the promotion of the use of energy from renewable sources.
Brussels, 23. 1.2008. COM（2008）19 final.

EU, 2010. Report from the Commission on sustainability requirements for the use of solid and gaseous biomass sources in electricity, heating and cooling.
http://eur-lex.europa.eu/LexUriServ/LexUriServ.do?uri=COM:2010:0011:FIN:EN:PDF.

EU, 2011. Assessing the Land Use Change Consequences of European Biofuel Policies 111pp. http://trade.ec.europa.eu/doclib/html/148289.htm.

European Environment Agency, 2011. Opinion of the EEA Scientific Committee on Greenhouse Gas Accounting in Relation to Bioenergy, 15 Sept. 2011.
http://www.eea.europa.eu/about-us/governance/scientific-committee/sc-opinions/opinions-on-scientific-issues/sc-opinion-on-greenhouse-gas/at_download/file.

Gillespie, E., 2008. Stemming the tide of 'Greenwash'. Consumer Policy Review, 18(3): 79-82.

Futerra, 2011. The seven Sins of Green-washing.
http://sinsofgreenwashing.org/index35c6.pdf

Fukushima, G., The Great Hanshin Earthquake.
http://www.jpri.org/publications/occasionalpapers/op2.html.

Hudiburg, T., Law, B., Wirth, C. and Luyssaert, S., 2011. Regional carbon dioxide implications of forest bioenergy production. Nature Climate Change, 1: 419-423.

IEEP, 2010. The Indirect Land Use Change Impact of the Use of Biofuels in the EU.
http://www.ieep.eu/assets/786/Analysis_of_ILUC_Based_on_the_National_Renewable_Energy_Action_Plans.pdf.

IPCC, 2007. Intergovernmental Panel on Climate Change, 4th Assessment. Summary for Policymakers. http://www.ipcc.ch/publications_and_data/ar4/syr/en/contents.html.

Keidanren, 2009. Voluntary Action Plan on the Environment. http://www.keidanren.or.jp/en/policy/2010/109.pdf.

METI, 2011. Detailed design considerations for Purchase of Renewable Energy. http://www.meti.go.jp/committee/summary/0004405/038_02_02.pdf.

METI, 2012. *Chotatsu kakaku iinkai* Committee report, 27 April.
http://www.meti.go.jp/committee/chotatsu_kakaku/pdf/report_001_01_00.pdf.

METI, 2012a. Announcement of Decision on FIT

system.
http://www.enecho.meti.go.jp/saiene/kaitori/kakaku.html.
METI, 2012b. Responses to the Public Comments. http://www.meti.go.jp/press/2012/06/20120618001/20120618001.html.
MOE, 2007. Japan's Green Purchasing Policy – tackling illegal logging. http://www.env.go.jp/en/earth/forest/pamph_jgpp.pdf.
MOE, 2012. Japan's GHG emissions. http://www.env.go.jp/press/file_view.php?serial=21128&hou_id=16054
National Policy Unit, 2012. Japan Rebirth Strategy. http://npu.go.jp/policy/pdf/20120821/20120821_en.pdf
Norton, M. and Aikawa, T., 2012. Stakeholder engagement in developing a sustainable biomass policy for Japan. International Journal of Environment and Sustainability, 1(4): 1-17.
Norton, M., 2010. Motivating Leaders towards Innovation in Sustainability – Shinshu University's 'GREEN' MOT. Innovation Management (6): 84-104.
Norton, M., 2012. Business and Sustainability- Duty or Opportunity. Routledge Publishers
ISBN 978-0-415-52933-3.
Nuffield Council on Bioethics, 2011. Biofuels: Ethical Issues. Nuffiels Council, London.
http://www.nuffieldbioethics.org/sites/default/files/Biofuels_ethical_issues_FULL%20REPORT_0.pdf.
Prime Minister's Office, 2011. Press Conference by Prime Minister Naoto Kan after G8 Summit. http://www.kantei.go.jp/foreign/kan/statement/201105/27G8naigai_e.html.
Royal Society, 2008. Sustainable Biofuels- prospects and challenges. Royal Society, London. http://royalsociety.org/WorkArea/DownloadAsset.aspx?id=5501.
Zanchi, G., Pena,N. and Bird, N., 2010. The upfront carbon debt of bioenergy. Joanneum Research. http://www.birdlife.org/eu/pdfs/Bioenergy_Joanneum_Research.pdf.

ANNEX: PRINCIPLES CONCERNING THE PROMOTION OF SUSTAINABLE USE OF BIOMASS ENERGY- ORIGINAL JAPANESE TEXT

日本におけるバイオマスの持続可能な利用促進のための原理・原則
～適切なFIT制度の設計のために～

2012年1月

提言文書

1. 背景

- 私たちは、地球規模で進行する気候変動の深刻な影響を回避するため、再生可能エネルギーの一つとして、バイオマスエネルギーの利用を国内外で積極的に進めるべきであると考え、このような動きを支持する。
- ただし、バイオマスエネルギーの特性を考慮し、持続可能な利用が行わなければならない。
- また、バイオマスエネルギーの利活用を推進する各種の政策も持続可能性についての配慮の下で利用が促進されるよう、科学的な分析に基づき、注意深く設計される必要がある。
- そこで、日本におけるバイオマスの持続可能な利用促進を目指す環境NGOらは、国内及び海外、特に欧州の最新動向の調査を行い、2回の円卓会議を開催して議論を行ったところ、以下の3つの原理・原則が必要であると合意し、本声明文を発表するに至った。
  - ➢ 真の意味でのGHG（温室効果ガス）の削減への寄与
  - ➢ 健全な生態系の保全
  - ➢ 経済・社会面での配慮
- なお、本提言文は、現在検討が行われている「再生可能エネルギー特別措置法（以下FIT制度）」の影響の大きさを鑑み、同制度において適切な設計が行われることを求めるものである[12]。
- 加えて、自由市場における民間レベルでの取組についても同様の原則に配慮することが期待される。
- また、推奨される取組には実現に時間を要するものも含まれているが、FIT制度は15年以

---

(12) バイオマスのエネルギー利用は、効率性等から熱利用がメインとなり、FIT制度内での配慮に加えて、熱利用の推進のための政策が別途必要である。

上の長期に渡る制度であることから、段階的な取組の蓄積により、理想に近づけていくアプローチが必要であると考えられる。
- ターゲットとしているのは、主に固体バイオマス、特に木質系バイオマスである。
- 国内で利用されるバイオマスには国産のものと、輸入によるものがあるが、本原則は同様に適応される。

2. 3つの原理・原則[13]

(1) 真の意味でのGHG（温室効果ガス）の削減への寄与
- バイオマスエネルギー利用促進の最も重要な目的は、GHG削減による気候変動対策である。したがって、バイオマスエネルギー利用促進施策の一つであるFIT制度も、その目的に沿って制度設計が行われなければならない。
- IPCC第4次評価報告書[14]によれば、2050年までの深刻な気候変動の危機を回避するためには、全地球レベルで向こう20-30年以内に抜本的なGHG削減が必要である。
- したがって、バイオマスエネルギーの利用は、このような気候変動の危機の回避のためにGHG削減に寄与するものでなければならない。

【炭素負債の発生の回避】
- バイオマスエネルギー生産を目的として森林の皆伐等を行うと、生態系から大量のGHGが排出され、樹木が成長して再び炭素を固定するには数10年から100年以上の時間を要するため、抜本的な気候変動対策が求められている向こう20-30年の間に「炭素負債（Carbon-debt）」が発生するため、単純に「炭素中立（Carbon-neutral）」と言う事は難しいと考えられるようになっている。
- そこで、バイオマスエネルギー利用に伴うGHG削減の算定方法は、土地利用段階から始まる全てのフェーズを含み、炭素負債を捕捉できるものでなければならない（フル・カーボン・アカウンティング・アプローチ）。

【地球規模でのGHG削減への寄与】
- バイオマスが地球規模で取引されている状況を踏まえて、GHG削減量は算定され、地球規模でのGHG削減へ寄与していることを確認する必要がある。
- つまり、現行の京都議定書のルールとは異なるが、バイオマスの生産国と消費国が異なる場合も、全てのフェーズを対象として、GHG削減量は計算されなければならない。

【エネルギー利用効率】
- バイオマスの利用チェーンのエネルギー効率（GHG削減効果）は、エネルギー転換後の利用のあり方（具体的には、熱か電気か、コジェネレーションか）により大きく変わるため、利用のあり方も考慮されなければならない。
- なお、一般的には、熱利用の効率は高く80%以上を実現するが、発電効率は良くて数10%であり、熱利用もしくはコジェネレーションが推奨される。

【推奨事項】
- このように、GHG削減への寄与を考慮した場合、以下のようなFITの制度設計及び関連方策が推奨される。
  ➢ GHG削減量の適切な計測と、最低基準の設定（欧州では、化石燃料比60%）
  ➢ 土地利用改変を伴わない既存の生産システムからの残材や余剰物の利用の促進
    ◇ なお荒廃地や耕作放棄地等の有効利用は是認されるが、こうした土地利用についても、健全な生態系の保全と利用の促進、経済的・社会的な貢献が配慮されるべきである。
  ➢ バイオマス輸送に必要なエネルギー量の配慮（輸送方法、距離／等）
  ➢ 熱利用を基本に、コジェネレーションの推進
  ➢ フル・カーボン・アカウンティングを可能とするLCAの研究推進及びデータの蓄積

(2) 健全な生態系の保全と利用の促進
- 生物多様性によりもたらされる生態系サービスの重要性が広く認知されるようになっている。日本も、生物多様性条約の批准や、v次に渡る生物多様性国家戦略の策定、名古

---

[13] 参加団体は枠組みとしての3原則に合意したが、以下は3原則に基づき議論された論点であり、個別論点については必ずしも参加団体の見解を反映するものとは限らない。
[14] http://www.ipcc.ch/publications_and_data/publications_ipcc_fourth_assessment_report_synthesis_report.htm

●論　文

図表：バイオマスのバリューチェーン

屋におけるCOPの開催など国際的な貢献を行ってきたところである。
- したがって、バイオマスエネルギー利用の基礎的な遵守事項として、バイオマスの生産が行われる生態系の健全性は保全、もしくは促進され、生物多様性は保全されなければならない。

【合法性の確保】
- 国の内外を問わず、関連する法令は遵守され、合法性が確保されなければならない。
- 国内においても、皆伐後の再造林の放棄が問題になっていることから、十分な確認が必要である。

【保護価値の高い生態系の保護】
- 保護価値や天然性が高く、炭素蓄積の高い生態系は破壊されてはならない。

【多様な生態系サービスとの調和】
- 既に人為的利用が行われている生態系も、生態学的な知見に基づき、（マテリアル及びエネルギー利用を含む）物質生産以外の多様な生態系サービスと調和した利用が行われなければならない。
- 伝統的に生態系サービスに依存してきた地域社会との対立を招くことを避けるために、土地所有者や利用権保有者だけではなく、地域住民や関連するステークホルダーの参加を得て、FPIC（Free, Prior and Informed Consent；自由で事前の情報に基づいた同意）を満たした、生産が計画されることが望ましい。

【推奨事項】
- このような健全な生態系の保全を考慮した場合、以下のようなFITの制度設計及び関連方策、民間での自主的な配慮が推奨される。
- なお、これらの原則は、マテリアル利用を目的とした森林利用における配慮事項と共通するものである。
  - 合法性の確保
  - 土地利用計画・森林計画等の中での、生態系保全や他の生態系サービスと調和可能なゾーニングと透明性の高い計画策定プロセス
  - 原料供給源の明確化と、サプライチェーンのトレーサビリティーの確保
  - 持続可能性の担保が可能な森林認証の普及、積極的な利用

（3）経済・社会面での配慮
- 本来バイオマスエネルギーの利用は適切に行われれば、エネルギーミックスの促進、農林業セクターの活性化などへの寄与も期待できるものである。
- 特に、FIT制度が国民の社会的な負担に基づき、運営される制度であることを考慮すると、エネルギー安全保障の向上、地域経済の活性化に寄与するような、統合的なアプローチが必要である。

【ガバナンスの強化】
- 本来期待される地域経済への好影響を実現させるためには、その基礎として、行政システム及び林業等の生態系サービス利用ビジネスの透明性・効率性の向上が必要である。
- 日本においては、伐採届けの未提出や再造林の放棄などの法律の形骸化や、林業の高コスト構造が問題となり、2009年末に発表された森林・林業再生プランなどによる改革が進んでいるところであるため、このような政策と連携した総合的な制度設計が求められる。

【地域単位での取組を促す小規模分散型利用の優遇】
- FIT制度における買取価格設定の基本的な考え方はコストベースであり、小規模分散型の利用を進めるために、電力の買取価格は、発電容量に合わせて設定されるべきである。
- また、規模が小さくとも高い効率を実現できるコジェネレーションに対して、何らかの優遇施策を設けるべきである。
- なお、本稿では触れないが、ドイツにおける再生可能エネルギー熱法など、熱利用を促進するための枠組みの検討が別途必要である[15]。

【推奨事項】
- このような経済的・社会的な貢献を実現する点から、以下のようなFITの制度設計及び関連方策が推奨される。
  - 出力規模別／利用形態別の買取価格の設定（小規模の優遇、出力規模の上限設定）
  - コジェネレーションへのボーナス
  - 合法性の確保（再掲）

➢ 森林・林業政策との統合[16]
  ➢ 持続可能性の担保が可能な森林認証の普及、積極的な利用（再掲）

---

(15) ドイツのFIT制度では、電力の買取価格は、発電容量の小さいものが高めに設定され、かつ対象となる発電容量に上限が定められているため、小規模分散型の利用が促進されている。また、規模が小さくとも高い効率を実現できるコジェネレーションに対して、ボーナスを用意し、小規模分散型の利用を促進している。
(16) 農林水産省では、2009年に「森林・林業再生プラン」を策定し、その中でもバイオマスエネルギー利用を推進している。

●論文

Manufacturing Engineering in Europe and Japan:
A Preliminary Comparative Case Study of Two Automotive Component Suppliers

Mihail Marinov

International Graduate School of Social Sciences
Yokohama National University
mihail-marinov-tv@ynu.ac.jp

Associate Professor Daniel Arturo Heller

International Graduate School of Social Sciences
Yokohama National University
daheller@ynu.ac.jp

Abstract: In recent years, Japanese manufacturers have been seeking to increase the supporting capabilities (e.g., product and process engineering) of their overseas production facilities. As a result, increased attention is being paid by both academics and practitioners to the tasks and functions of manufacturing engineering, and how these tasks and functions may be transferred overseas. However, compared to Japan and the United States, we could find few academic works in English or Japanese that address the tasks and functions of manufacturing engineering in Europe. In an effort to address this hole in the literature, this paper compares and contrasts the tasks and functions of manufacturing engineering in a European automotive component supplier with that of a Japanese supplier of a similar automotive component. Taking a descriptive approach, the paper draws from existing manufacturing engineering literature on the known tasks and functions of manufacturing engineers. Our preliminary comparative case study suggests that, at least prescriptively, the tasks and functions of manufacturing engineering in Europe, while containing important differences, are largely similar to what is found in Japan. This finding contrasts with what has been revealed in the literature regarding the largely different tasks and functions of manufacturing engineering in the U.S. and Japan. The paper concludes by outlining how the research presented in this paper may be further developed going forward.

Keywords: new product development, production engineering, concurrent engineering, simultaneous engineering, manufacturing, automotive component supplier, comparative case study

1. Introduction

There is renewed practical and theoretical interest in how companies can improve the productivity of their existing production lines and introduce new production lines more efficiently (Jonsson et al., 2004; Nakaoka et al., 2005; Shibata, 2009), both of which are primary responsibility of manufacturing engineers (Shibata, 2009; Whitney et al., 2007; Koike, 2008). This interest is particularly high in Japan, where companies are increasingly focusing on the transfer of manufacturing engineering processes to overseas facilities, now that the transfer of production processes to overseas plants has become more routine (Shibata, 2009).

Previous research findings substantiate this renewed attention on manufacturing engineering. After conducting an analysis of new product development, manufacturing engineering and production processes in manufacturing companies, Eisenhardt and Tabrizi (1995) and Leonard and Sensiper (1998) argue that the use of cross-functional teams and concurrent engineering may improve technology transfer, innovation and time to market.

The importance of integration across functions has been pointed out in research on new product development (Clark and Fujimoto 1991, Wheelwright and Clark 1992, Adler 1995), and it has also been stressed that the successful integration of groups with different functions can be difficult. Moreover, Wheelwright and Clark (1992) argue that new product development is an activity that should involve all the different functions that exist in a company, and go on to assert that the choice of communication medium, direction, frequency and timing that is used to integrate the contributions of the diverse participants can largely determine whether this integration is successful or not.

New product development in the Japanese auto industry has been one of the principal objects of research on inter-functional integration. Fujimoto (1999, 2003, 2007) and Aoshima (2001a, 2001b) point out that there is much overlapping of tasks and personnel in the new product development of Japanese automakers, as well as a constantly high level of cross-functional integration. Also, product managers in Japanese companies tend to exert a particularly high level of influence over other participants in product development projects (Clark and Fujimoto, 1991; Higashi and Heller, 2012). Regarding integration in downstream processes like manufacturing, Koike (1994), Pil and MacDuffie (1999), Shibata (1999, 2001) among others, assert that production workers in Japanese companies integrate production skills with troubleshooting skills.

Compared with the volume of literature on the tasks and functions of new product development projects and manufacturing plants, there is little research that addresses the tasks and functions of manufacturing engineering. The importance of the tasks and functions of manufacturing engineering has been pointed out by Nakaoka et. al. (2005), however, it is difficult to find detailed research on the tasks and functions of manufacturing engineering, with a few notable exceptions (described below) that tend to focus on Japan in general, and Toyota in particular.

Shibata (2009) presents a comparative study on the tasks and functions of manufacturing engineers in Japan and the United States (based on nine Japanese and three American companies in different industries). Koike (2008) examined the tasks and functions of manufacturing engineers in a single Japanese automobile manufacturer (presumably Toyota). Whitney et al. (2007) studied the role of manufacturing engineering in door engineering and door assembly at Toyota. Murase (2007) also examined manufacturing engineering in Toyota and its role in knowledge creation. Murase (2011) conducted a comparative study of manufacturing engineering in Toyota and Honda.

Shibata (2009) points out that one of the unresolved questions for future research is the study of manufacturing engineering in countries other than Japan and the United States. Since we could find little research in English or Japanese on the tasks and functions of manufacturing engineers in another important and historically strong manufacturing region, namely Europe, the present paper uses a field-based comparative research approach to conduct a preliminary investigation of how manufacturing engineering is done on this continent.

This paper provides, firstly, a comprehensive review of the literature on the tasks and functions of manufacturing engineers. Secondly, the paper focuses on revealing the tasks, functions and organization of manufacturing engineers in a European supplier of automotive components, and comparing them with what is found in a Japanese supplier of similar automotive components. We analyze the similarities and differences in the manufacturing engineers' tasks and functions, including the location of the workplace of manufacturing engineers (i.e., within plants, R&D centers, or headquarters).

The findings from our preliminary comparative case study suggests that, at least prescriptively, the tasks and functions of manufacturing engineering in Europe are largely similar to what is found in Japan. Differences were found in the allocation of responsibility among manufacturing engineers and the timing of the participation of production workers in new product development projects.

2. Literature review

2.1 What is manufacturing engineering? (Tasks and Functions)

Shibata (2009) researched nine Japanese and three American companies and concludes that the manufacturing engineers in these companies perform the

following four main tasks:
(1) Line design - designing production lines or production processes;
(2) Method development - developing production methods, machinery, and/or equipment;
(3) Production preparation - preparing the manufacturing of new products, such as setting up new production machinery or equipment, making jigs, tools and dies, managing trial production, writing operations manuals, instructing workers on production operations, and stabilizing mass production;
(4) Production improvement - improving existing production lines, processes, machinery, equipment, jigs, tools, and/or dies, with the aim of getting productivity increases.

According to Shibata (2009), these four tasks require the fulfillment of two functions that are important for the success of the work of manufacturing engineers:
(1) Smooth and efficient mediation between product design (engineering) processes on one side, and production processes on the other side.
(2) Significant improvement in productivity that cannot be achieved simply by continuous improvements (kaizen) performed by production workers.

Koike (2008) indicates that in the single Japanese company that he studied, manufacturing engineers are broadly divided into two types - *seisan-gijutsu-sha*, who are mainly responsible for work related with the design of assembly lines, as well as the development of production facilities (upstream processes), and *seizo-gijutsu-sha*, who are mainly responsible for work related with manufacturing trials and production ramp-up (downstream processes). In his study on manufacturing engineering in Toyota's press shop, Murase (2007) confirms these findings and asserts that the tasks and functions of *seizo-gijutsu-sha* can be described as focused on operation, while the tasks and functions of *seisan- gijutsu-sha* can be described as focused on knowledge.

In Shibata (2009) the above-mentioned Japanese phrases are translated as follows - *seisan-gijutsu-sha* as manufacturing design engineers, who correspond to manufacturing engineers in American companies, and *seizo-gijutsu-sha* as production process engineers, who roughly correspond to manufacturing technicians in American companies. For the sake of clarity, this paper uses the English wording adopted by Shibata (2009) (for Europe, the American equivalents are used).

2.2 Why focus on manufacturing engineering?

In the academic literature, the involvement of production workers in improving the efficiency and effectiveness of Japanese production facilities has been highlighted as one of the factors in the success of Japanese production systems (MacDuffie and Pil, 1997). For example Liker (2004) argues that Toyota fosters production employee involvement at upper levels. Shibata (2009), while not denying the important role played by production workers, clarifies that in addition to production workers, manufacturing engineers play important roles in production processes in Japanese companies. Specifically, Shibata (2009) argues that production process engineers who are highly involved in manufacturing engineering work contribute to the overall efficiency and effectiveness of the production systems in Japanese companies. In addition, Shibata (2009) asserts that production systems in Japan are supported by the participation in upstream processes by engineers who work primarily in downstream processes. Extending this argument, one might argue that the tasks and functions of manufacturing engineering, notably production process engineers, and the involvement of downstream employees in upstream processes, rather than difficult to understand work concepts such as teamwork and kaizen, is what actually forms the critical supporting structure for Japanese production systems and contributes to their high efficiency and effectiveness.

2.3 Types of work organization in manufacturing engineering

According to Shibata (2009), in the nine Japanese firms of his study, the tasks and functions of manufacturing engineers is organized in the following three types:

First type (mainly assembly and part-processing shops - automobiles, car components, electronics): divisions of manufacturing design engineers (located in their headquarters) were in charge of (1) line design, (2) method development, and some parts of (3) production preparation; divisions of production process engineers (located in each plant or business unit) were in charge of other types of tasks related to (3) production preparation and (4) production improvement.

Second type (mainly material-processing shops - semiconductor-related, steel): divisions of manufacturing design engineers for (1) line design and some parts of (3) production preparation; divisions of production process engineers are in charge of other types of tasks related to (3) production preparation and (4) production improvement, and divisions of equipment engineers for (2) method development.

Third type (semiconductor, ceramics, chemistry): divisions of manufacturing engineers (including both manufacturing design engineers and production process engineers) are in charge of (1) line design, (3) production preparation, and (4) production improvement. Former divisions, now outside equipment makers, conduct (2) method development. In this type, the main task of the manufacturing engineering divisions was production improvement by the production process engineers.

In the three American companies, the tasks and functions of manufacturing engineers are organized in the following two types:

First type (mainly assembly and parts-processing shops - car/machine components): divisions of manufacturing engineers are in charge of the four tasks, i.e. (1) line design, (2) method development, (3) production preparation, and (4) production improvement.

Second type (mainly material-processing shops - ceramics): divisions of manufacturing engineers are in charge of (1) line design, (3) production preparation, and (4) production improvement; a division of equipment engineers is in charge of (2) method development.

In the three American companies, the manufacturing engineers and the manufacturing technicians are members of the manufacturing engineering divisions. The manufacturing engineers conducted decision-making in their offices, which were far from the plants. The manufacturing engineering work is actually done by the manufacturing technicians, who work close to the plant shops and get instructions from the manufacturing engineers.

2.4 Manufacturing design engineers and production process engineers in a Japanese automobile manufacturer

Koike (2008) performed an in-depth study of a Japanese automobile manufacturer (a careful reading of the paper suggests that the manufacturer is Toyota as the paper is about a Japanese company and it mentions NUMMI, a joint venture between Toyota and GM that closed in 2010). According to Koike (2008), the manufacturing design engineers are responsible for (1) line design - designing new production lines and making changes to existing production lines, and (2) method development - developing machinery and equipment. The production process engineers are responsible for (3) production preparation and (4) machine troubleshooting and dealing with quality problems after volume production has begun. Manufacturing design engineers and production process engineers do the following at each stage the manufacturing process:

(1) Product engineering. Main role - product engineers. Manufacturing engineers (manufacturing design engineers and production process engineers) make suggestions regarding the design of new products. Plants are represented by teams of production process engineers and production workers who make written proposals concerning product design. These proposals can be accepted or rejected by the product engineers.

(2) Assembly line design. Main role - manufacturing design engineers. This stage starts almost at the same time as the product engineering stage. At this stage manufacturing design engineers:

a) determine the basic structure of the line; production process engineers and production workers participate too, especially in the detailed design of the assembly process;

b) select the manufacturers of the equipment;

c) determine the number of people necessary to operate the assembly line.

(3) Production facilities manufacturing and testing. Main role - manufacturing design engineers. Production process engineers participate too.

(4) Manufacturing trials. Main role - production process engineers. During this stage, meetings are held every day on the shop floor with a wide range of participants - production process engineers, manufacturing design engineers, product engineers and production workers. Koike (2008) explicitly states that the participation of production workers in this stage is an important characteristic of Japanese companies.

(5) Production ramp-up. Main role - production process engineers. Production workers actively participate in this stage too.

(6) Volume production. Production process engineers and production workers are responsible for troubleshooting.

2.5 Industry-specific characteristics of manufacturing engineering

Shibata (2009) points out that there are differences in the tasks and functions of manufacturing engineers in the nine Japanese and three American companies according to three industry types: assembly, parts-processing (parts, such as car or electronic components, are cut, pressed, and/or shaped in the shops), and material-processing shops (industrial materials, such as chemical or steel materials, are reacted, smelted, and/or rolled in the shops). The differences are as follows:

(1) Engineering of production lines or processes - manufacturing engineers in the assembly and parts-processing shops make blueprint drafts for new production lines, while manufacturing engineers in the material-processing shops, using existing production lines, decide the process sequences, the methods by which materials will react, and the condition under which the new products will be manufactured.

(2) Frequency of introduction of new production lines - manufacturing engineers in assembly shops more often introduce new production lines than manufacturing engineers in parts-processing and material-processing shops. In addition, manufacturing engineers, assistant, and first-line supervisors, and/or production workers in assembly shops more often improve existing production lines than in parts-processing and material-processing shops.

(3) Involvement in research & development or product design - the role of manufacturing engineers in research & development or product design performed in material-processing shops is bigger than the role of manufacturing engineers in research & development or product design performed in assembly and parts-processing shops.

2.6 Differences between manufacturing engineering in Japan and USA

Regarding differences between manufacturing engineering in Japanese and American companies, Shibata (2009) concludes that there are two characteristics in the nine Japanese companies of his research that "do not exist or are weak" (p. 1906) in the three American companies:

(1) inter-divisional tasks and functions of production process engineers; Shibata (2009) refers to the work of the production process engineers in the Japanese companies as "organized inter-division work" (p. 1906) and claims that organized inter-division work contributes to the performance of the Japanese production systems.

(2) the involvement of employees engaged in the downstream stages of the production process with work related to the upstream stages.

As for the division of labor in the work of manufacturing engineers, Shibata (2009) found that in the nine Japanese companies there is a horizontal division of labor between the manufacturing design engineers (*seisan-gijyutsu-sha*) and the production process engineers (*seizo-gijyutsu-sha*). Production process engineers in the nine Japanese companies are responsible for the organization and control of production preparation and consequently this stage of the production process, i.e. production preparation, receives a more clearly defined shape. In the three American companies, maintenance workers belonging to their respective unions play similar roles and have similar responsibilities as the production process engineers in the nine Japanese companies.

As for the division of labor in the manufacturing engineering work in the three American companies, the finding is that there is a vertical division of labor between the manufacturing engineers and the manufacturing technicians. There is a clear difference between the "directive work of the manufacturing engineers" and the "hands-on work of the manufacturing technicians" (p. 1906). The vertical division of labor between manufacturing engineers and manufacturing technicians found in the three American companies seems to derive from "a traditional dichotomy of vocational culture in the United States" (p. 1906) which can trace its history back to the Industrial Revolution in the 19th Century.

2.7 Interactions between downstream and upstream processes

Research and development is the first stage of the manufacturing processes, followed by product design, manufacturing engineering and finally production (Shibata, 2009). This flow of work is where the second characteristic of manufacturing engineering work in the nine Japanese companies, namely the interactions between upstream and downstream manufacturing processes, is to be found. In relation to this, Fujimoto (1999, 2003, 2007) points out that the transfer of information between upstream and downstream processes is important. Shibata (2009) supports this conclusion of Fujimoto and claims that, regarding the different stages of the manufacturing processes, in Japanese companies downstream employees are heavily involved with work in upstream processes in the following two ways:

(1) from the manufacturing engineering processes to the research and development or product design processes;
(2) from the production processes to the manufacturing engineering processes.

This conclusion is supported by Koike (2008), who indicates that in the single Japanese company of his research, the tasks and functions of manufacturing design engineers (mainly responsible for upstream processes) considerably overlap with the tasks and functions of production process engineers (mainly responsible for downstream processes). Also, at the product engineering stage, manufacturing design engineers make suggestions regarding the design of new products.

Furthermore, Shibata (2009) maintains that such an interaction between upstream and downstream new product development processes leads to concurrent engineering and "shortens the lead-time of new product development, and reduces the times of trial production" (p. 1907).

Also, there are interesting indications from Whitney et al. (2007) that for example at Toyota, manufacturing engineering acts like a bridge between manufacturing (downstream) and product design (upstream), connecting them and making them communicate smoothly, seeking to reconcile their often conflicting interests and thus contributing to performance improvement. Whitney et al. (2007, p. 11), found that manufacturing engineering at Toyota "considers manufacturing variation and its effect on the (design performance) targets. Variation can arise in any (manufacturing) domain (e.g., press, paint, assembly)...", and manufacturing engineering "has taken on the role of negotiating among these domains before going back to engineering design with suggestions".

According to Whitney et al. (2007) the role of the manufacturing engineering department, at least in the body engineering part of Toyota's new product development process, is to be a pro-active interface between the product design department and the manufacturing department, thus playing the role of a systems integrator. Moreover, based on a research on Denso, a company that follows the Toyota Production System (Anderson, 2003), Whitney (1995) argues that Denso's strength is not strictly limited to manufacturing but rather Denso excels in the way it links manufacturing with new product development.

2.8 Why is manufacturing engineering in Japan different from manufacturing engineering in the United States?

Shibata (2009) explains the difference between the tasks and functions of manufacturing engineers in Japan and the United States with the following two orientations that tend to characterize Japanese companies:

(1) Integration (*suriawase*) orientation, and
(2) Production workplace orientation.

First, regarding the orientation towards integration, it is necessary to point out that according to Fujimoto (2003, 2007) product architecture can be broadly divided into two types: integral product architecture and modular product architecture. Compared with overseas companies, Japanese companies tend to possess higher capability to manufacture products with integral architecture. Automobiles are a typical example of products with integral architecture. Thus, Japanese companies in the automobile industry can benefit from their integral orientation.

Shibata (2009) confirms the findings of Fujimoto and asserts that in the nine Japanese and three American firms of his research, "not only assembly and parts-processing firms, such as automobile firms, but material processing firms in Japan have higher integral capabilities and are strongly oriented to integration" (p. 1907-1908). This description of the product architecture orientation of companies in Japan seems to be different from the description of American companies, which are characterized as "oriented towards segregation" (p. 1908). According to Shibata (2009), an important requirement for companies which are oriented towards integration is the employment of production workers who, in addition to production skills, also possess troubleshooting skills. The conclusion of Shibata (2009) is that the tasks and functions of manufacturing engineers are supported by the human resource management systems in Japanese companies.

Examples given in Shibata (2009) that show the orientation of Japanese companies towards integration include:

(1) Middle-up-down decision making performed

by assistant and first-line supervisors.

(2) Mediating roles between product design (or research and development) and production processes performed by manufacturing engineers.

(3) Involvement of downstream employees with work and tasks associated with upstream processes.

Second, as for the production workplace orientation, Shibata (2009) states that in the nine Japanese companies, "everybody, from top executives to the lowest employees, is heavily oriented to production and production workplaces" (p. 1908). The usual practice in the nine Japanese companies is that managers and employees perform their tasks at the actual workplace where they can easily observe and participate in various activities. These activities include on-site problem solving and the concept known in Japanese as *genchi genbutsu* (actual place, actual thing). According to Liker (2004) Toyota has adopted the same concept too.

As a typical aspect of the *genchi genbutsu* concept, the actual production workplace is the training place where new employees, who have just graduated from universities and who are going to work as product engineers or manufacturing engineers, learn by watching what is actually being done at the *genba* (shop floor). In relation to this point, Shibata (2009) observes that assistant and first-line supervisors are often responsible for the education and the training of new engineers at the nine Japanese companies, which is a practice that cannot be observed at the three American companies in his research. Shibata (2009) concludes that the strong orientation towards the production workplace, which can be described as typical for Japanese companies, "organizes production process engineers near the production workplaces, and induces the production process engineers to conduct their production preparation and improvement work in the production workplaces thoroughly" (p. 1908).

2.9 Segregation of engineers and production workers in the United States

Bechky (2003a, 2003b) conducted research on the relationships between people and tangible objects at production workplaces, from which some conclusions regarding the segregation (as opposed to integration) of engineers and production workers can be drawn. The research was conducted at an American company, and it is based on the fact that machines can be touched and felt, which means that machines are "tangible objects". According to Bechky (2003a), one of the important characteristics of tangible objects is that they create common ground that helps reconcile misunderstandings between people or groups of people. In this American company, these groups of people are engineers, technicians and assemblers (production workers), and each group represents "a different work context with distinct understandings of the product and the production process" (p. 317).

Bechky (2003a) found that the contrast in work context was greatest between engineers, "who rarely touched or even saw the machines while focusing on drawing their designs" (p. 317) and assemblers, who spent all of their time at the production workplace. However, Bechky (2003a) states that at least in the American company he studied, engineering drawings are not considered to be "tangible objects". Thus, engineering drawings had the effect of separating the engineers, and to a lesser degree the technicians, from the assemblers. The technicians were separated to a lesser degree because their work context is placed between the engineers and the assemblers and it "overlapped that of the other two groups" (p. 317). The level of importance and high professional position of the engineers were strengthened by the complex language of the engineering drawings.

Shibata (2009) supports Bechky's conclusion and asserts that at least in the three American companies in his research, manufacturing engineers "believe that they grasp production and production workplaces more thoroughly than production supervisors and workers" (p. 1908). Also, it seems that the engineers do not visit the production workplaces very often. The result is that in the production workplaces of the three American companies machines cease to function as Bechky's (2003a) "tangible objects".

In contrast to the American cases, in the nine Japanese companies studied by Shibata (2009), the production workplace is where production process engineers usually do their job and spend much of their working time. In addition, according to Shibata (2009), a considerable number of supervisors and workers are given support to learn how to do machine troubleshooting and how to understand engineering technology, such as engineering drawings. As a consequence, it can be argued that in the nine Japanese companies physical objects such as machines, products and components, and even conceptual objects, such as engineering drawings, function as Bechky's (2003a) "tangible objects" and serve as common ground that can reconcile differences among groups. Shibata (2009) concludes that the integral capabilities of the Japanese production workplaces are supported and reinforced by the above-mentioned tangible objects and by the fact that engineers and production workers learn from each other.

3. Methodology

Building on Shibata (2009), we employ a comparative case study methodology, utilizing qualitative data obtained through in-depth interviews in a European supplier of automotive components and a Japanese supplier that makes similar automotive components. All of the components we studied at both suppliers are largely mechanical, used in the same major subsystem of an automobile (i.e., powertrain, chassis, body, and interior) and have an impact on safety and perceived quality. The components can be described as "black-box parts" (Clark and Fujimoto, 1991) that require co-development and integration (*suriawase*) between a supplier and an automaker.

We interviewed personnel who fit our working definition of manufacturing engineering: engineers who are primarily responsible for tasks that can be described as "in-between" product design and manufacturing (e.g., modifying or suggesting modifications to a product engineering drawings to better fit with existing equipment in a plant or plants). This working definition is similar to that used in Whitney et al. (2007) too, although in this particular paper the term, production engineering, is used.

As our object of analysis, we have selected two suppliers that occupy similar positions in the value chain of the auto industry. This research design allows us to identify and illuminate similarities and differences, not only in the observed characteristics of manufacturing engineering in each of the two companies, but also in the search for possible explanations of these similarities and differences. Since we control for industry-specific characteristics, we are able to obtain a greater understanding of the processes that are standard and those that are country-specific and/or firm-specific, which has important implications for the transferability of the overall conclusions of the research. At the present preliminary stage of this research, our comparison focuses on describing the work characteristics (tasks and functions) of manufacturing engineering in a European supplier of automotive components and a Japanese supplier that makes similar automotive components.

The next step is to try to understand why these two suppliers have formed different or similar work characteristics of manufacturing engineering and to seek to identify and explain both the differences and the similarities. This approach allows the research to go beyond description and towards the more fundamental goal of explanation. The overall aim of this research is to add to the existing body of knowledge on manufacturing engineering, with particular attention paid to the under-researched subject of the tasks and functions of manufacturing engineering in Europe. At this stage of the research we can pose a rather simplistic but basic research question: *What are the tasks and functions of manufacturing engineering in a European supplier of auto parts?* A Japanese supplier of similar auto parts provides a good basis for comparison because there is a decent amount of research on the tasks and functions of manufacturing engineering in Japanese automotive companies.

The qualitative data used in this present paper to compare the manufacturing engineering in a European supplier of automotive components (Supplier E) and a Japanese supplier who makes similar automotive components (Supplier J) comes from the following first-hand sources. One or both of the authors visited a European plant and the adjacent R&D center of Supplier E twice, in June 2011 and January 2012, and closely observed the production process of automotive component on two assembly lines, during which time we also conducted interviews with manufacturing engineers. We also visited another R&D facility of Supplier E in September 2011, during which time we held numerous discussions with a director of manufacturing and participated in a phone discussion with a manufacturing engineer of this company. During the third visit (January 2012), the first author and another accompanying researcher conducted an interview with the head of the manufacturing engineering section of the R&D center. Follow-up email correspondence was also conducted with the same employee in September and October 2012.

We visited a Japanese plant of Supplier J in June 2012, where we observed the production process of the automotive component and interviewed some of the local managing staff, one of whom had an extensive background in manufacturing engineering at Supplier J. We visited another plant of Supplier J in Japan and its headquarters in August 2012, where we observed the production process of the automotive component again and interviewed the head of the manufacturing engineering department and four other manufacturing engineers. We made a follow-up visit to the headquarters of Suppler J in September 2012 and talked with the head of the manufacturing engineering department and three other manufacturing engineers.

4. Preliminary findings from the comparative case study

The preliminary findings of our study on the tasks and functions of manufacturing engineers in Suppliers E and J generally confirm the conclusions of Shibata (2009) regarding the main tasks that are carried out by manufacturing engineers, namely line design, production method development, production preparation and production improvement. The manufacturing engineers in Suppliers E and J also perform these main tasks and functions.

Regarding the organizational structure of manufacturing engineering in Supplier E, manufacturing engineers and manufacturing technicians work in a R&D center which is located next to a plant where the automotive components are made. Product engineers who design standard components work in the same R&D center, as well as product engineers who are responsible for the customization of standard components. The aim of the customization is to make changes in the design of standard components in order to provide the best fit with each customer's requirements. Product engineering for standard and customized components is done in separate departments, and manufacturing engineering for standard and customized components is separate too, however all of them are directly subordinated to the manager of the R&D center, a product engineer. So, we can say that for the automotive components we studied in Supplier E, manufacturing engineering is part of research and development.

Manufacturing design engineers (*seisan-gijyutsu-sha*) in Supplier J work in the headquarters of that company, however, the headquarters is located next to a plant where automotive components are made. In addition to the manufacturing design engineers in the headquarters, there are two groups of manufacturing design engineers in two large-scale plants in Japan. In the organization of Supplier J manufacturing design engineers are part of the research and development division, together with technology planning, cost planning, and product engineering.

Manufacturing technicians in Supplier E are in the same R&D center, together with the manufacturing engineers. Also, there are manufacturing technicians in every plant of Supplier E who are integrated into a section belonging to the plant management and/or integrated into a workshop team on the plantfloor, depending on the size of the plant.

Production process engineers (*seizo-gijyutsu-sha*) at Supplier J are in the department of the manufacturing design engineers at the headquarters, as well as in production control sections, which are found in every plant of Supplier J. In larger plants, production process engineers form their own subsection in the production control section, while in smaller plants they are simply part of the production control section without forming a subsection of their own. However, regardless of the number of production process engineers and their formal organizational subordination, they always work closely with the manufacturing design engineers who are located at the headquarters of Supplier J and the two large-scale plants.

Regarding interactions between upstream and downstream new component development processes, in Supplier E before the start of a new component development project, manufacturing engineers usually hold meetings and discuss different aspects of the new project with product engineers. Interactions between upstream and downstream processes are facilitated by the fact that the desks of product engineers and manufacturing engineers are in the same office room. In one case the desks actually face each other. This change to co-locate was made in the late 2000s. According to one of the manufacturing engineers, sharing the same boss (i.e., the manager of the R&D center) made "working together harder in the beginning, but better."

As already mentioned, product engineers, manufacturing engineers and manufacturing technicians in Supplier E are located in the same R&D center. For each new project related to the development of a new standard component, a design leader in charge of product engineering is nominated and paired with a manufacturing engineering leader in charge of line design and production method development. These two people are a product engineer and a manufacturing engineer respectively, and both of them receive support from other employees who are members of the same team and whose work is associated with downstream processes, like manufacturing technicians. All of these participants work together closely and hold meetings on a regular basis.

Manufacturing engineering leaders in Supplier E are responsible for product quality improvement, cost reduction and achievement of higher manufacturability of new standard components. To facilitate the abovementioned improvements, a workshop is held after the new product drawings have been made. During this stage, the new product drawings are not frozen and not approved for manufacturing yet. The workshop is held in two phases and its duration is 3 or 4 days in theory. The manufacturing engineering leader is in charge of this team, and its members encompass a wide range of employees including, for example, manufacturing engineering, purchasing, quality control, maintenance, and when possible, line operators. The participation of line operators in the workshops depends on their availability. So, the involvement of the most downstream employees is prescribed as a preference. In addition, manufacturing technicians participate in FMEA (failure modes and effects analysis).

In Supplier J, manufacturing design engineers (*seisan-gijyutsu-sha*) as well as production process engineers (*seizo-gijyutsu-sha*) participate together with product engineers in FMEA and product and process reviews that are conducted within new component development projects to help identify potential design problems based on past experience with similar products or processes, or based on common failure mechanism logic, enabling the development team to design those failures out of the component with the minimum of effort and resource expenditure, thereby reducing development time and costs. The participation of production process engineers in FMEA is based on their experience and knowledge of potential problems that may occur during manufacturing. Production process engineers take part in line design and production method development, which is an area of responsibility of manufacturing design engineers, and in product design reviews, which are done before but sometimes concurrently with or after FMEA. Manufacturing design engineers and production workers (line operators) also participate in FMEA and design reviews.

Any other requests from the plant (i.e., production process engineers) regarding manufacturability, quality, cost, easy maintenance of equipment, etc. for new products, first go through the manufacturing design engineers who act like a filter, and then reach product engineers who take these requests into account when making the engineering drawings of new products. Dies are an exception; only manufacturing design engineers make proposals related to manufacturability, cost and quality. Production process engineers do not participate in the development of dies.

During the line design phase and the production method development phase, the manufacturing engineers in Supplier E perform the *lead role*, that is to say coordinate and strongly influence decision making in these phases, which among others includes decisions related to cost, cycle time, machine efficiency, number of operators, layout of the line, specific performance indicators like mean time before failure (MTBF), etc. This lead role played by manufacturing engineers also extends to execution of the majority of the tasks in the line design phase and the production method development phase, which among others include mechanical, electrical and software development for production equipment, equipment validation and acceptance, etc.

In Supplier E, during the line design phase and the production method development phase of a new component development project, the focus of participation of the manufacturing technicians who are co-located in the R&D center is on providing *technical support* to manufacturing engineers. This *technical support* encompasses analytical tasks such as methods-time measurement, R&R (repeatability and reproducibility) studies, calculation of run-at-rate for the equipment acceptance phases, etc. Subsequently, manufacturing technicians in plants play the *lead role* in the production preparation phase, that is to say coordinate and strongly influence decision making and execute the majority of the tasks in this phase which among others include equipment setting-up, validation and acceptance of the new manufacturing process in the plant, writing operation manuals and standardized work sheets for operators, training workers, etc..

Manufacturing engineers in Supplier E are responsible for line design and production method development, and they deliver to equipment suppliers specifications, such as performance targets, number of line operators, etc. The design and manufacturing of the equipment is outsourced but the manufacturing engineers of Supplier E are responsible and actively participate in equipment design, testing, and validation (see below), and their responsibility continues down to production preparation (management of manufacturing trials, line installation, operator training, etc.) and production ramp-up. In fact, although manufacturing technicians at the plant play the lead role in the production preparation phase, a manufacturing engineer at the plant has the overall responsibility for production preparation. The *main task* and responsibility of manufacturing technicians in plants is productivity improvement during volume production.

A similar distribution of *lead roles* along the different phases of the new component development project between manufacturing design engineers and production process engineers was observed in Supplier J, as well. Thus, in Supplier J manufacturing design engineers have the *lead role* during the line design phase and the production method development phase and their responsibility continues down to production ramp-up.

In Supplier J, the *main task* of production process engineers is equipment maintenance during volume production, but they also execute tasks related to continuous improvement (kaizen) and give full consideration to problems related to usability of equipment and potential manufacturing defects in the products. In executing these tasks, during the line design phase and the production method development phase, the focus of production process engineers' participation is on giving *informational support* to the manufacturing design engineers providing them with feedback from the point of view of the line operators. It is also necessary to mention that plant maintenance personnel are included within the organization that holds the production process engineers.

In Supplier J production process engineers actively participate in production preparation and production ramp-up. However, the weight (or level of responsibility) of manufacturing design engineers gradually starts to decrease from the manufacturing trials phase, at the same time the weight of production process engineers gradually starts to increase. This finding is largely in agreement with the first type of work organization of manufacturing engineering in Japanese companies described by Shibata (2009), where the tasks and functions of manufacturing engineering in production preparation are shared by manufacturing design engineers and production process engineers.

In Supplier E, manufacturing engineers are responsible for development of production methods (assembly sequence, etc.) but they usually do not develop or manufacture machines and equipment, although they are closely involved in this process. The manufacturing of machines and equipment is outsourced to equipment suppliers. Supplier E has a commitment from the suppliers to dedicate the necessary staff for the development and manufacturing of the equipment. Checking the allotment of resources and the outsourcing of tasks is another important role that manufacturing engineers in Supplier E perform. Visits to the supplier are made every 2 weeks during the development phase, every month in the beginning of the building phase, and every 2 weeks at the end of the building phase. During the setup phase Supplier E personnel work constantly at the supplier's plant. Personnel from the supplier work constantly at Supplier E during the installation and validation phase. Good relations between engineers on both sides is important. There is daily communication during the whole time.

In Supplier J, manufacturing design engineers develop production methods too, but in addition they also develop machinery and equipment together with the equipment suppliers. The manufacturing of large equipment is outsourced to equipment suppliers, however smaller equipment is manufactured in-house.

5. Conclusions, limitations, and future research directions

The aim of this research is to examine the tasks and functions of manufacturing engineering in a European supplier of auto parts, and to compare these tasks and functions to those in a Japanese supplier of similar auto parts in order to identify similarities and differences between the two companies with regard to manufacturing engineering. By doing so the research seeks to add to the existing literature on manufacturing engineering by advancing our understanding of how manufacturing engineering is done in Europe.

Due to the preliminary nature of the findings, at this stage it is not possible to give a definitive and detailed answer to the question about tasks and functions of manufacturing engineering in Supplier E and Supplier J. Nevertheless, our current preliminary findings are summarized in Figure 1.

The major difference between the tasks and functions of manufacturing engineering in Supplier E and Supplier J appears to be in the area of responsibility

FIGURE 1 JAPAN'S ELECTRICITY GENERATION BY ENERGY SOURCE TO 2010

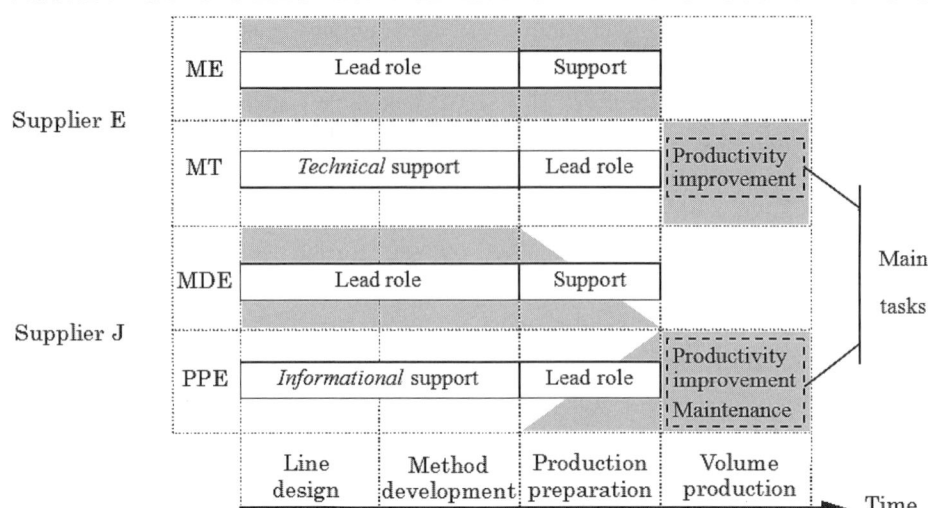

Figure Key:
ME - manufacturing engineers; *MT* - manufacturing technicians; *MDE* - manufacturing design engineers; *PPE* - production process engineers; *Grey color* - overall responsibility; *Lead role* - coordinate and strongly influence decision making and execute the majority of the tasks in the phase; *Technical support* - focus on analytical tasks in the phase; *Informational support* - focus on providing feedback from the point of view of the line operators: *Support* - provide various forms of technical and/or informational assistance.
Notes:
1. At Supplier J, in the production preparation phase overall responsibility is shared between MDE and PPE, with MDE's level of responsibility gradually *decreasing* as the phase progresses and PPE's level of responsibility gradually *increasing* as the phase progresses.
2. This figure omits the product engineering phase for simplicity reasons, which starts before the line design phase and during which product engineers have overall responsibility and perform the lead role.
3. This figure amalgamates production ramp-up into production preparation for simplicity reasons.
4. This figure shows the different phases in sequential order for simplicity reasons, although in reality the phases are overlapped at both companies.

of manufacturing technicians and production process engineers respectively. In Supplier E, the focus of participation of manufacturing technicians in the line design phase and the production method development phase is on providing *technical support* to the manufacturing engineers by executing some of the analytical tasks associated with these two phases. While in Supplier J, the focus of participation of production process engineers in the line design phase and the production method development phase is on providing *informational support* to the manufacturing design engineers, a sort of liaison between the plants and R&D. Unlike what was found in Supplier E, in Supplier J equipment maintenance is an another important task executed by production process engineers. In Supplier J we also observed that in the production preparation phase overall responsibility is shared between manufacturing design engineers and production process engineers.

Even at this early stage of our research it seems that in Supplier E interactions between production workers and manufacturing engineers on one side, and product engineers and manufacturing engineers on the other, are prescribed in a way not noticeably different from how these interactions are prescribed in Supplier J, in that both companies prescribe involvement of production workers in upstream processes. However, the way production workers are prescribed to become involved appears to be different. At both Supplier E and Supplier J production workers are prescribed to become involved from the product engineering phase, when the new product drawings are being validated for manufacturing. However, at Supplier E production workers become involved through a single workshop event that covers both the product engineering phase and the line design phase. Whereas, at Supplier J, they are prescribed to become involved preferably from the beginning but certainly from the first FMEA and DR of the project. This involvement is not a single event but typically occurs multiple times.

In addition, we do not know the extent to which this prescribed preference is actually realized in Supplier E. Also, Supplier E and Supplier J are similar in the organization of manufacturing engineering because in both companies the manufacturing engineers are part of their respective new product development divisions. The status of manufacturing technicians in Supplier E remains an important ongoing line of inquiry in this research.

Another finding that shows similarities between Supplier E and J is the location of their manufacturing engineering divisions. The divisions of both companies are located near plants, which is in striking contrast to what Shibata (2009) observed in the United States, where the divisions of manufacturing engineers are located far from the plants. In the case of Supplier J, the plant that is near the headquarters is relatively old (for Supplier J), and so is the equipment. However, we know that in the case of Supplier E, the company recently relocated product and process engineering, including the manufacturing engineering division, near a plant, as part of a recent operational realignment.

Supplier J on the whole does not deviate considerably from what Shibata (2009) found about manufacturing engineering in Japanese companies. There is considerable interaction between downstream and upstream processes at Supplier J, and the involvement of production process engineers extends up to product engineering through the participation of production process engineers in the product design review and FMEA.

The deliberate choice of two suppliers of similar automotive component for analysis, while necessary for the particular purpose of this study, is of course a limitation of the research. In relation to the specific case studies, the lack of more detailed information with regard to the tasks and functions of manufacturing engineering, such as that which could be obtained through a questionnaire survey for example, rendered it difficult to measure the extent of manufacturing engineering's interaction with new product development and production.

Like all research, this study has unearthed other questions. The possibility exists to continue to deepen the findings of this paper and explore any other important attributes and characteristics that might underpin and determine manufacturing engineering in other companies both in Japan and overseas. Furthermore, recognizing the importance of historical, economic and socio-cultural circumstances as influencing factors in the development of manufacturing engineering, the opportunity exists to explore these areas further, and to broaden our understanding of their influence on manufacturing engineering.

Moreover, the performance implications of differences in the functioning of manufacturing engineering, such as time compression (shorter lead time) and manufacturing cost reduction, may provide researchers with another promising avenue of approach to understand the importance of manufacturing engineering and, for example, the degree to which manufacturing engineering of Japanese companies can and should be transferred to their overseas affiliates.

Finally, this research focuses on just one country in Europe, so there is need to establish the degree to which this case is representative of other auto suppliers in this country. A next step could then be to see how the functions of manufacturing engineering in this country compare with other countries in Europe. Additional studies of different companies and industries in Europe and Japan would be a valuable exercise and would help define the external validity of this research.

If further research finds that the functions of manufacturing engineering in Supplier E are typical in Europe then another question may arise: how such a European work context can be expected to impact efforts by Japanese manufacturers as they increasingly expand the functions of their European facilities to include an increased role of manufacturing engineering at their local site.

6. Acknowledgements

The authors would like to thank the practitioners at the two suppliers who kindly cooperated and still continue to cooperate with this research. Appreciation is also expressed to Daniel E. Whitney who commented on an earlier draft and the two anonymous reviewers for their constructive comments and suggestions that greatly contributed to improving the paper. We would also like to thank Takefumi Mokudai, Tomoki Kaji and Marina Kido, for their kind cooperation during the company visits. Of course, the authors take full responsibility for any errors or omissions.

（2012年10月1日投稿、12月11日受理）

REFERENCES

Adler, P. S. (1995). Interdepartmental interdependence and coordination: The case of the design/manufacturing interface. *Organizational Science*, vol. 6, no. 2, March-April 1995, pp. 147-168.

Anderson, E. (2003). The enigma of Toyota's competitive advantage: Is Denso the missing link in the academic literature?, *Pacific Economic Paper*, no. 339, Australia-Japan Research Centre.

Aoshima, Y. (2001a). "Nihon-gata Seihin-kaihatsu Purosesu to Konkarento Enjiniaringu: Boingu 777 Kaihatsu Purosesu tono Hikaku", [The Japanese Style of New product development and the Computer-based Concurrent Engineering: A Comparison with the Boeing 777 Development Process], in *Chishiki to Inobeshon*, [*Knowledge and Innovation*], ed. Institute of Innovation and Research, Hitotsubashi University, Tokyo: Toyo Keizai, pp. 25-49 (in Japanese).

Aoshima, Y. (2001b). "Shin-seihin Kaihatsu no Manejimento", [Management of New product development], in *Inobeshon Manejimento Nyumon*, [*Introduction to Innovation Management*], ed. Institute of Innovation and Research, Hitotsubashi University, Tokyo: Nihon Keizai Shimbunsha, pp. 151-187 (in Japanese).

Bechky, B.A. (2003a). Sharing Meaning across Occupational Communities: The Transformation of Understanding on a Production Floor. *Organization Science*, vol. 14, no. 3, pp. 312-330.

Bechky, B.A. (2003b). Object Lessons: Workplace Artifacts as Representation of Occupational Jurisdiction. *American Journal of Sociology*, vol. 109, no. 3, pp. 720-752.

Clark, K. B., & Fujimoto, T. (1991). *Product Development Performance*, Harvard Business School Press, Boston, MA.

Eisenhardt, K. M., & Tabrizi, B. (1995). Accelerating adaptive processes: Product innovation in the global computer industry. *Administrative Science Quarterly*, vol. 40, March 1995, pp. 84—110.

Fujimoto, T. (1999). *The Evolution of a Manufacturing System at Toyota*, Oxford: Oxford University Press.

Fujimoto, T. (2003). "*Noryoku Kochiku Kyoso: Nihon no Jidosha Sangyo wa Naze Tsuyoi no ka*", [*Capability Building Competition*], Tokyo: Chuokoron Shinsha (in Japanese).

Fujimoto, T. (2007). *Competing to Be Really, Really Good*, Tokyo: International House of Japan.

Higashi, H., & Heller, D. A. (2012). Thirty Years of Benchmarking Product Development Performance: A Research Note. The University of Tokyo Manufacturing Management Research Center, Discussion Paper Series, No. 395.

Jonsson, D., Medbo, L., & Engstrom, T. (2004). Some considerations relating to the reintroduction of assembly lines in the Swedish automotive industry. *International Journal of Operations & Production Management*, vol. 24, no. 8, pp.754-772.

Koike, K. (1994). Learning and Incentive Systems in Japanese Industry, in *The Japanese Firm*, eds. M. Aoki and R. Dore, Oxford: Oxford University Press, pp. 41-65.

Koike, K. (2008). "*Kaigai Nihon Kigyo no Jinzai Keisei*", [*Human Resources Development of Japanese firms overseas*], Tokyo: Toyo Keizai Shinbunsha (in Japanese).

Liker, J.K. (2004). *The Toyota Way: 14 Management Principles from the World's Greatest Manufacturer*, New York: McGraw-Hill.

Leonard, D., & Sensiper, S. (1998). The role of tacit knowledge in group innovation. *California Management Review*, vol. 40, no.3, spring 1998, pp. 112-132.

MacDuffie, J. P., & Pil, F.K. (1997). Changes in auto industry employment practices: An international overview, in *After Lean Production*, eds. Thomas A. Kochan, Russell D. Landsbury and John Paul MacDuffie. Cambridge: MIT Press, 1997, pp. 9-44.

Murase, M. (2007). "Toyota Seisan Hoshiki ni okeru Chishiki Souzou to Seisan Gijutsu: Puresu Kanagata no Tenkai o Jirei to shite", [Knowledge creation and Production engineering in the Toyota Production System: Development of the press die as an example]. "*Osaka Sangyo Daigaku Keiei Ronshu*", [*Osaka Sangyo University Journal of Business Administration*], vol. 9, no. 1, pp. 47-71 (in Japanese).

Murase, M. (2011). "Jidosha meika no Keiei-infura to shite no Seisan Gijutsu ni kansuru Kenkyu: Toyota to Honda ni okeru Puresu Gijutsu no Hatten o Chushin to shite", [A Study on Production Engineering as a Business Infrastructure of Automobile Manufacturers: Focusing on the Development of Press Technology in Toyota and Honda], Summary of Ph.D. Thesis, "*Osaka Sangyo Daigaku Keiei Ronshu*", [*Osaka Sangyo*

University Journal of Business Administration], vol. 12, no. 3, pp. 365-369 (in Japanese).

Nakaoka, T., Asao, U., Tamura, Y., and Fujita, E. (2005). "Shokuba no Bungyo to Henka to Ijo eno Taio", [Division of Labor on the Manufacturing Shopfloor: The Division of Labor to Deal with Changes and Problems on Production Sites], "*Nagoya Shiritsu Daigaku Jimbun Shakai Gakubu Kenkyu Kiyo*", [*Journal of Humanities and Social Sciences of Nagoya City University*], vol. 18, pp. 1-51 (in Japanese).

Pil, F. K., & MacDuffie, J.P. (1999). Transferring Competitive Advantage Across Borders: A Study of Japanese Transplants in North America, in *Remade in America: Transplanting and Transforming Japanese Production Systems*, eds. Liker, J.K., Adler, P. and Fruin, M. New York: Oxford University Press, pp. 39-74.

Shibata, H. (1999). A Comparison of Japanese and American Work Practices: Skill Formation, Communications, and Conflict Resolution. *Industrial Relations*, vol. 38, no. 2, pp. 234-260.

Shibata, H. (2001). Productivity and Skill at a Japanese Transplant and Its Parent Company. *Work and Occupations*, vol. 28, no. 2, pp. 192-214.

Shibata, H. (2009). A comparison of the roles and responsibilities of manufacturing engineers in Japan and the United States. *The International Journal of Human Resource Management*, Vol. 20, No. 9, September, pp. 1896-1913.

Wheelwright, S. C., & Clark, K. B. (1992). *Revolutionizing New Product Development: Quantum Leaps in Speed, Efficiency and Quality*. The Free Press, New York.

Whitney, D. E. (1995). Nippondenso Co. Ltd.: A Case Study of Strategic Product Design, in *Engineered in Japan*, eds. Liker, J. K., Ettlie, J. E. and Campbell, J. C., Oxford: Oxford University Press, pp. 115-151.

Whitney, D.E., Heller, D.A., Higashi, H., & Fukuzawa, M. (2007). Production Engineering as Systems Integrator? - A Research Note based on a Study of Door Engineering and Assembly at Toyota Motor Corporation, The University of Tokyo Manufacturing Management Research Center, Discussion Paper Series, No. 169.

フラッグキャリアの「生産調整」について
―1990年代から2000年代にかけてのBAヨーロッパ路線―

信州大学経営大学院

教授　柴田　匡平

1. 問題の所在

90年代に進展したメガ・アライアンスの中核ペアをなす欧米の大手航空会社のうち、ヨーロッパ系フラッグキャリアにとって、ニューヨーク路線は大きな意味をもつ。メガ・アライアンスはニューヨーク-自社ハブ路線を重視するヨーロッパ系フラッグキャリアと、自社ハブ（内陸ハブ）-ヨーロッパ首都の路線を拡充したい米系メガキャリアによる市場分割の性格をもつが、前者の「後背地」であるヨーロッパ域内では、2000年代初頭からLCC（Low Cost Carriers）が台頭著しく、従来型のフルサービス・キャリアは苦戦が伝えられる。

よく知られるように、LCCのビジネスモデルは徹底した低コスト追求にもとづく価格破壊により、従来はVFR（Visiting Friends and Relatives）あるいはバジェット・トラベラーズと呼ばれてきた層の掘り起こしを狙うものである。低コスト追求の方策は、典型的には統一機種、短距離（最大区間距離2000km程度）、単一クラスの高密度座席配置、機内アメニティの有料化（いわゆるノーフリル）、インターネットなどの直接予約、座席指定と発券の撤廃、非組合型の労働力、大都市周辺部の二線級空港の活用、チェックイン・カウンターや搭乗方式の簡素化などど。顧客に訴求するのはまずもって低価格である[1]。しかしその一方では、エアクラフト・エコノミクス（機種固有の経済性）と空港事業所経費の効率化を追求する観点から、ターンアラウンド・タイム（到着から出発までの時間）を切り詰めて高稼働するので、頻度が高くなる。高頻度すなわち便の多さは、乗り継ぎを想定しない旅客にとって利便性を提供する。単に低価格というよりも、その座席数の多さが既存大手にとって脅威になるのである。

いっぽう既存のフラッグキャリアにとって今や競争は多層的になった。顧客基盤である短距離路線網でのLCCによる価格破壊に加え、「ヨーロッパの玄関」をめぐるアライアンス間の競争、ないしハブ間競争が起きているからである[2]。LCCによる破壊的イノベーションが2000年以降に伸長するなか、フラッグキャリアのビジネスモデルも再構築の局面にあるように思われる。それはブランドないしポジション見直しの契機にもなっているのではないか。

規制緩和がひきおこすこうした競争激化にさらされた既存大手航空会社が、個別の路線でどのような対応をとるか、具体的な変化を検証した論考はほとんど見当たらないようである。だがLCCの台頭による短距離路線への影響は、自社路線網への資源配分に影響を及ぼすだろう。エアラインが供給するのは座席と考えれば、LCCに優位性がある短距離路線では、供給効率の低下をいかに食い止めるかが課題になると思われる。すなわち生産調整が要請されるのではないか。その一方で、アライアンスは個別路線の社内における位置づけの見直しを要請すると考えられる。ハブ・アンド・スポーク方式を維持しようとするなら、短距離路

---

(1) LCCの価格政策いわゆるアラカルト・プライシングについては、中条潮『航空幻想―日本の空は変わったか』中央経済社、2012、*pp*.24-25、杉山純子『LCCが拓く航空市場―格安航空会社の成長戦略』成山堂、2012、*pp*.55-58ほか。
(2) 既存大手の短距離路線における二律背反的な位置づけについては拙稿「短距離路線の憂鬱―英国航空の国内・ヨーロッパ路線網―」信州大学経済学論集第41号、1999、*pp*.1-32；「ヨーロッパの玄関」をめぐる競争については拙著『ブリティッシュ・エアウェイズの経営1981-2010―民営化・国際展開とアエロポリティクス』中央書院、2011、第10章第4節、*pp*.183-186.

線には一定の「下限」が想定されるだろう。ヨーロッパにおけるハブ間競争において、特には対米路線からの乗り継ぎを確保する必要があるからだ。いずれのばあいでも、航空会社による座席数の配置は各社の政策を反映するはずである。そこで、国際民間航空機関ICAOの統計（ser. TF, Traffic Flow）をもとに、イギリスのフラッグキャリアであるブリティッシュ・エアウェイズ（BA）の大型路線における変化を簡単に追跡したい。しかし資料上の制約があるので、その点をまず整理する。

依拠するser. TFはICAOに対し国際航空各社が毎年の運航状況を報告した数値をまとめた年次統計で、路線別・機種別の便数、提供座席数、搭乗客数、座席利用率、提供有償荷重、貨物運送量、郵便運送量が示されている。しかし路線は都市間で、複数の空港があるばあいは合計値である。

第2に、報告は悉皆的ではなく、エアラインによって欠落がある。社内での数値取りまとめにかなりのコストがかかるためと推測されるが、たとえば著名なLCCであるライアンエア（アイルランド）はほとんど報告しない。したがって路線（都市間）での運航状況と実績は、数値報告を済ませたエアラインについてしか分からず、全体の競合状況とはみなせない[3]。

第3に、印刷媒体を用いたser. TFは2001年分の冊子を最終とし、以後の数値はインターネット上のデータベース（ICAOdata.com）として提供されている。冊子体では出発都市別に整序されていたので、当該都市からの全路線が一覧でき、各社の市場カバー率も推定できたが、現在は出発地・到着地と年次を入力せねば数値を得られないため、どのエアラインがどの都市からどこに運航しているかは極めて把握しにくくなっている。

また冊子体では未報告のエアライン名が記載されていたので、少なくとも乗り入れていることは分かったが、現在では未報告の場合には社名そのものが表示されないため、未報告なのか運航していないのか、データ上は不明である。加えて、冊子体ではダイバージョン運航にその旨の符号が付されていたが、現在では定期運航との区別を便数から推定するしかない[4]。

ser. TFは国際路線別、業者別の数値を時系列的に把握できる恐らく唯一の公開統計とみられるが、以上の制約があるため、短期に限定した分析には向かない。しかしほぼ継続的に報告するエアラインの長期的な推移の概容は、ある程度まで把握できると思われる。

2. NYC路線におけるヨーロッパ系フラッグキャリアの運航状況

Fig.1はメガ・アライアンスを形成したヨーロッパ系フラッグキャリアのニューヨークから各社の拠点空港への年間座席数推移である。すなわちKLMオランダ航空（KL）はアムステルダム便（AMS）、ルフトハンザ航空（LH）はフランクフルト便（FRA）、エールフランス（AF）はパリ便（PAR）、ブリティッシュ・エアウェイズはロンドン便（LDN）である。ニューヨーク-自社ハブ間は4社にとって戦略的な路線であり、2001年時点での各社の国際線RPKに占めるシェアを推定すると、KLが約8％（ロサンジェルスに次いで2位）、LHが約10.9％（1位）、AFが13.2％（1位）、BAが12.7％（1位）である[5]。

こうした市場に「当社便の座席」として提示し販売する席数は、当該路線（市場）に対する航空会社の政策を反映すると考えられる。またアライアンス内部では共に運航する路線での供給調整が行われる。したがって、各社のアライアンス相手

---

(3) ただし報告することによるエアライン側のメリットは疑問である。従来の市場分析はCRS（Computer Reservation Systems, or Global Distribution Systems）の予約データを加工したMIDT（Marketing Information Data Tapes）や社内データにより行なわれてきたが、MIDTは高額・大量なために十分な処理・分析能力をもつエアラインは大手に限られると言われる。Cf. Paul Clark, *Buying the Big Jets*, 2nd ed., Ashgate, 2007, p.42. いっぽうではインターネット経由による直接予約の比率が高まっており、80年代にくらべ運航データを開示しないエアラインは増えている。路線網（アライアンス）同士の競争はシステム競争として情報戦の色彩も帯びつつあり、プロバイダとの協業も展望されている。Cf. Nawal K. Taneja, *The Passenger Has Gone Digital and Mobile*, Ashgate, 2011.

(4) 現行のデータベースで便利な点として、かつては未報告のエアラインについて後年の冊子付録を参照する必要があったのが、随時に更新される点が挙げられる。しかし研究者の観点からすれば冊子体のほうが一覧性に富み、情報量も格段に大きかったことは否めない。なお後述する2002年以降の各社の値にはダイバージョンを含んでいる可能性があるが、補正できない。

(5) この数値は2010年（暫定値）では各社とも激減している。LHが2.8％、AFが5.1％、BAが8.5％、KLは不明である。対米オープンスカイ協定の発効（2008年3月末）により米国内への乗り入れ先が増えたのか、あるいは従来の遠距離国際線に注力したのか、別稿の課題としたい。

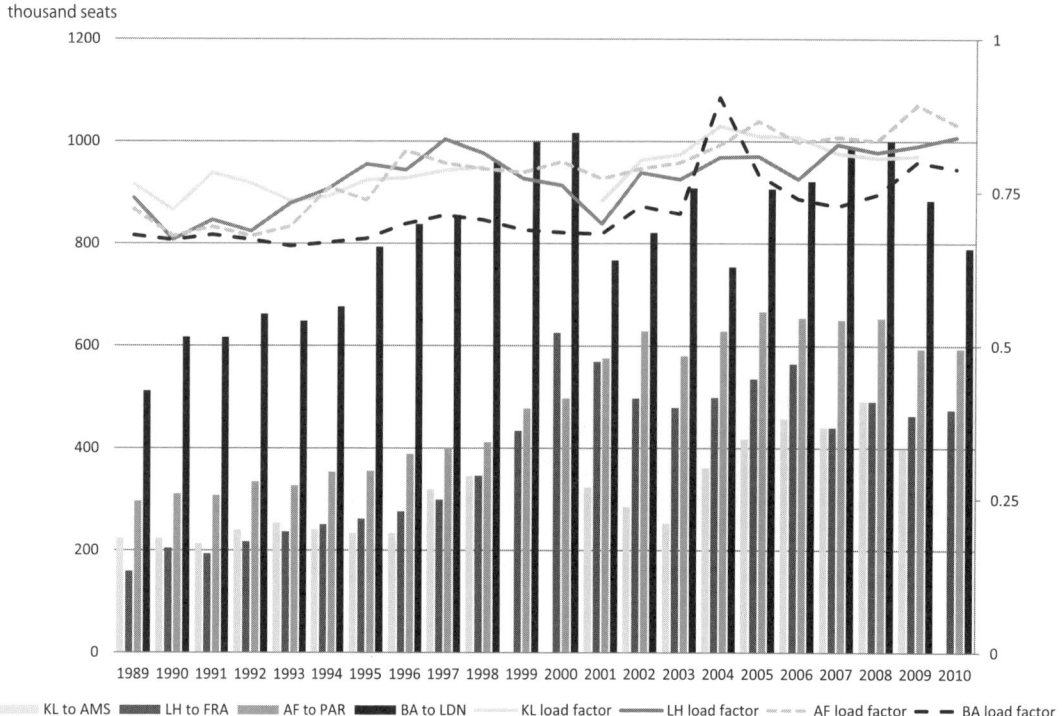

Fig. 1 Major European flag carriers' available seats from New York to their hubs 1989-2010

の便の提供座席数も考慮する必要がある。そこで、アライアンスが米独禁法適用除外を獲得した年次以降にはコードシェアを行なったものとみなし、追加してある[6]。なおKLのばあい、米側パートナーの運航量（コンチネンタル航空とノースウエスト航空合算）は自社便をやや上回る。またLHおよびAFのアライアンス相手の運航量はいずれも3分の1以下なのに対し、対象期間のBAはアメリカン航空とのコードシェアが英米当局に認められなかったため単独である。したがって、仮にアライアンス相手の分を除去すると、4社の棒グラフは格差が大きくなる。折れ線グラフは座席利用率（右軸）である。

各社ともにほぼ同じ傾向で推移しているが、BAのロンドン便の相対量が小さくなっていることが注目される。これはヨーロッパ域内および対米規制緩和と、機材・運用面での技術革新により「ヨーロッパの玄関」をめぐる争いが激化してい

ることを示唆する。ヨーロッパ域内で1997年に斉一的な自由化が達成されたのち、2007年にはEUによる対米オープンスカイ協定が締結され、航空運輸に関する二国間協定ネットワークは域内およびEU-米間では消滅した。機材の運用面では航続距離の延伸とイートップスの拡大により双発機の運航自由度が増し、4発機でなくともアメリカ内陸からの北大西洋路線の運用が可能になっている[7]。ニューヨークからみたロンドンは長きにわたり「ヨーロッパの玄関」だったが、90年代末からパリ、フランクフルト、アムステルダムが伸長を遂げ[8]、あらたな域内・域外の乗り継ぎ中心地が形成されつつある事情を反映するものと思われる。

座席利用率を見ると、各社とも長期的には漸増している。しかしBAのロンドン便は2004年を例外として、一貫して明らかに低いのに対し、KLとAFは近年80％後半に達し、スピル（溢出需要）

---

(6) KLについては96年〜2009年までノースウエスト航空便を、および2004年〜2010年はコンチネンタル航空便を加えてある。なお1999年、2000年、2010年についてはKLが報告していないため値が不明である。LHは2000年以降のシンガポール航空便を、AFには2000年以降のデルタ航空便を加えてある。なおser. TFでは運用者別の記載で、コードシェアを反映しない。

(7) ETOPS: Extended Twin Operationsについては、Clark, *op.cit.*, pp.162-168.

(8) *cf.* Graeme Leach, *Air Warfare*, IoD Policy Paper, Institute of Directors, Dec. 2000; CAA, "Connecting passengers at UK airports", Nov. 2008, p.15 Table 3-7.

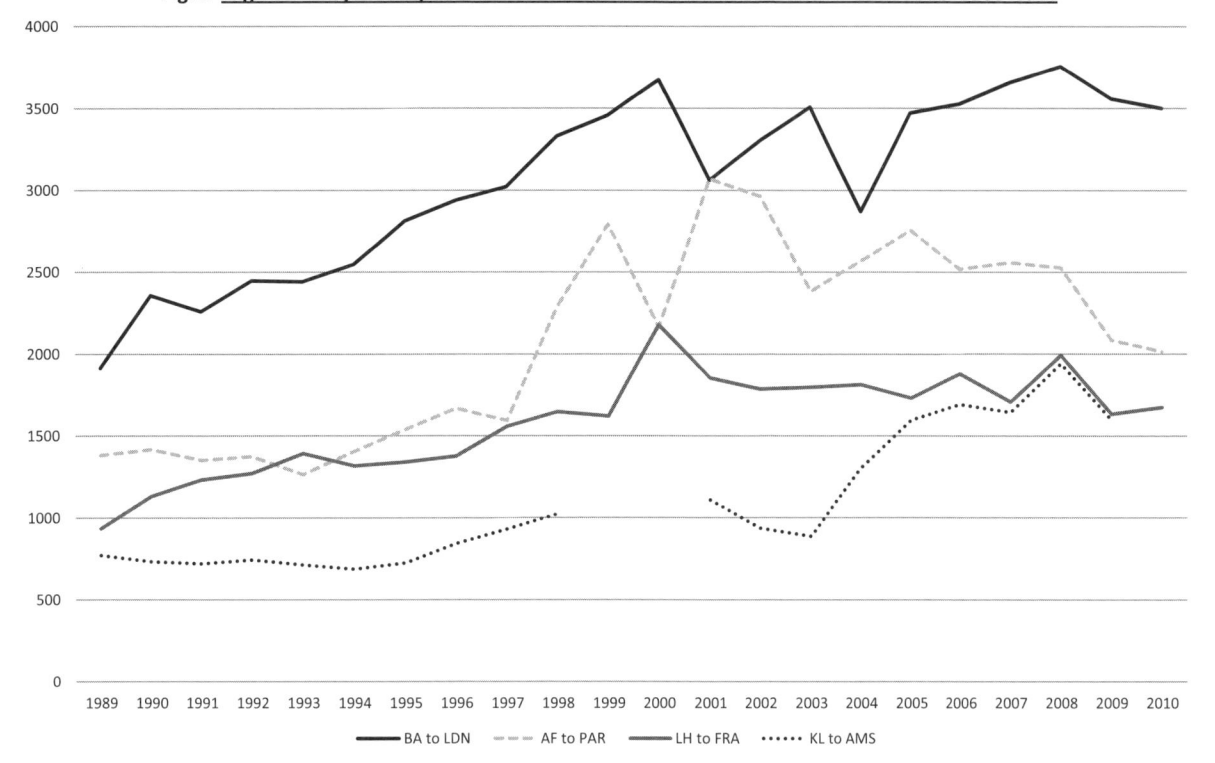

Fig. 2　Flights of major European carriers on the routes from New York to their hubs 1989-2010

――― BA to LDN　---- AF to PAR　――― LH to FRA　······ KL to AMS

が発生する水準ではないかと思われる[9]。04年のBAの高座席利用率は明らかに減便（Fig.2）の影響で、大量のスピルが発生したと推定される。

Fig.2は各社の便数で、順位、傾向ともFig.1の座席数とほぼ同断だが、頻度はビジネス客にとっての利便性を代理する指標とみることもできるだろう。Fig.1でみたように、提供座席数ではAFパリ便がBAロンドン便に近付いているものの、頻度の比はあまり変わっていない。これはAFがやや大型機材を運用する傾向があるためである[10]。つぎにヨーロッパ域内の状況をみよう。

3. BAのヨーロッパ便

Table 1は2000年におけるロンドン発BA便で座席数の多い乗り入れ先の上位11都市が、2010年にはどうなったかを示す。表中の比は座席数のそれである。なおニューヨークが同社最大の座席量になったのは97年で、それまではパリが最大だった。

2000年前後のBAは87年の民営化以後の拡大期にあたり、ヨーロッパ域内では独仏国内に現地子会社の路線網を展開し、フランチャイズや子会社群の積極展開がピークを迎えた頃である[11]。2010年はアメリカン航空との北大西洋路線でのコードシェアと収入プール契約を含む提携が14年越しに認可され（7月）、翌年にはイベリア航空との経営統合（2011年1月）がなされるなど、ワンワールドが実質化する時期である。

Table 1をみると、パリの急減が目立つっぽう、アムステルダムがある程度踏みとどまっている点が注目される。以下では、アライアンスで競合あるいは提携するヨーロッパ大陸系各社のハブとのあいだの路線を検討する。すなわちパリ路線（AF、スカイチーム）、フランクフルト路線（LH、スター・アライアンス）、アムステルダム路線（KL、スカイチーム）、マドリード路線（IB、ワンワールドで提携）をとりあげるが、ハブ同士を結ぶ路線は単なるスポークとは異なる位置づけになると思われ、本ノートでの仮説を簡単に整理す

(9) スピルについてはClark, *op.cit.*, pp.63-71. LCCやチャーター便はともかく、ビジネス旅客を主とするFFP会員の顧客基盤を涵養したい既存大手にとって、満席は必ずしも歓迎できない事象である。座席利用率は市場への適合度を示す指標ではあるが、通年で8割台の後半なら逸失売上が発生すると思われ、既存大手としては、ある程度の非効率を忍ばねばならない。
(10) 2009年の平均座席数はBAが249席、LHが284席、AFが285席、KLが249席。
(11) 詳細については拙著（2011）、第7章および第8章。

Table 1. BAの主な乗り入れ先へのロンドン出発便提供座席数および便数（2000、2010年）

都市　（区間距離km）	2000　座席数（便数）	2010　座席数（便数）	比
ニューヨークNYC　（5,540）	1,019,835（3,690）	774,275（2,998）	0.76
パリPAR　（347）	919,630（5,821）	430,015（2,723）	0.47
フランクフルトFRA　（654）	550,655（3,004）	340,118（2,931）	0.62
マドリードMAD　（1,245）	632,902（3,707）	287,721（2,040）	0.46
ミラノMIL　（936）	486,037（2,769）	370,594（3,020）	0.77
ローマROM　（1,443）	612,136（3,505）	426,426（2,514）	0.70
ストックホルムSTO　（1,462）	471,174（2,827）	307,860（1,862）	0.65
ジュネーブGVA　（753）	430,329（2,751）	360,932（2,772）	0.84
アムステルダムAMS　（370）	590,217（4,353）	551,879（4,264）	0.94
ロサンジェルスLAX　（8,759）	365,339（　883）	307,399（　958）	0.84
バルセロナBCN　（1,147）	476,935（2,693）	386,718（2,533）	0.81

出所：ICAO, *Digest of Statistics*, ser. TF, 2000; ICAOdata.comから算出。子会社およびフランチャイジー便を含む。

る。

　ある都市がスポークの乗り入れ先（スポーク都市と呼ぶ）として魅力的である条件を考えると、当該都市から他社のハブへの便が少ないか、あるいは皆無なばあい（地理学でいえば上位都市への従属性が強いばあい）、魅力は大きいであろう。しかしスポーク都市が競合他社のハブだと、当社のハブを経由する旅客量は、当社の路線網の充実度（乗り入れ先および頻度）と、相手方の路線網の充実度との勝負になる。両社の路線網が重複し、頻度や価格にあまり差がなければ、当社のハブを経由する旅客量は小さい。相手も同様だから、ハブ同士を結ぶ区間では乗り継ぎ客よりも、当該区間単独で搭乗する旅客、いわゆる起終点需要の比率が高まる。ところがこの区間の距離が小さければ、つまりハブ同士が近ければ、LCCが参入する蓋然性は大きい。

　逆に彼我の路線網に重複が少ないなら、今度はハブ同士を結ぶ路線での旅客争奪が主な課題になる。だが重複が少ないなら競争よりも協業のほうが合理的なわけで、アライアンスの契機である。そのさい、ハブ同士を結ぶ路線をどちらが主に運航するかは、当該路線の相対的重要度によるだろう。欧米間のメガ・アライアンスは、お互いの路線網に重複が少ないことが必要条件である。路線網の重複が少ないとは、しばしば両社のハブ間の距離が大きいことを含意する。

ロンドン-パリ路線

　パリ路線は長きにわたりBAにとって最大の座席数を提供する路線だった。ピークは1993年の123万席（6059便、旅客数82万人弱）だが、その後はほぼ一貫して低下している（Fig.3）。AFのピークは不明だが、89年以降ほぼ一貫して減少している。両社とも90年代後半に急減しており、これには94年開業の英仏海峡トンネルが大きな影響を与えたと考えられる。年間950万人（2010年実績）をカートレイン輸送する大動脈で、英仏間の交通を革命的に変えたからである。BAは提供座席数がピークに達した93年には1日17便を提供したが、24時間営業で15分おきの頻度を誇り、自家用車ごと英仏海峡を横断する利便性には太刀打ちできないだろう。イージージェットが1日3便程度と、大した頻度を提供しないのも、バジェット・トラベラーズというセグメントがトンネル利用層と重複するためと思われる。

　さて区間距離が短く、LCCが就航し、交通モード面での競合があり、しかもパリ-ニューヨーク便がどんどん増強されるとなれば、パリ-ロンドン間は、BAにとって、自社プレミアムクラスを利用する顧客層を運送できる程度でよいはずである[12]。ただしパリ-ニューヨーク間のプレミアム旅客（主に米系か）は子会社オープンスカイズに狙わせる[13]。事情はAFも同様で、ロンドン便よりもニューヨーク以下の対米便に注力するほうが合理的だ。オープンスカイズに対しては、頻度で圧倒する戦術と思われる。

●研究ノート

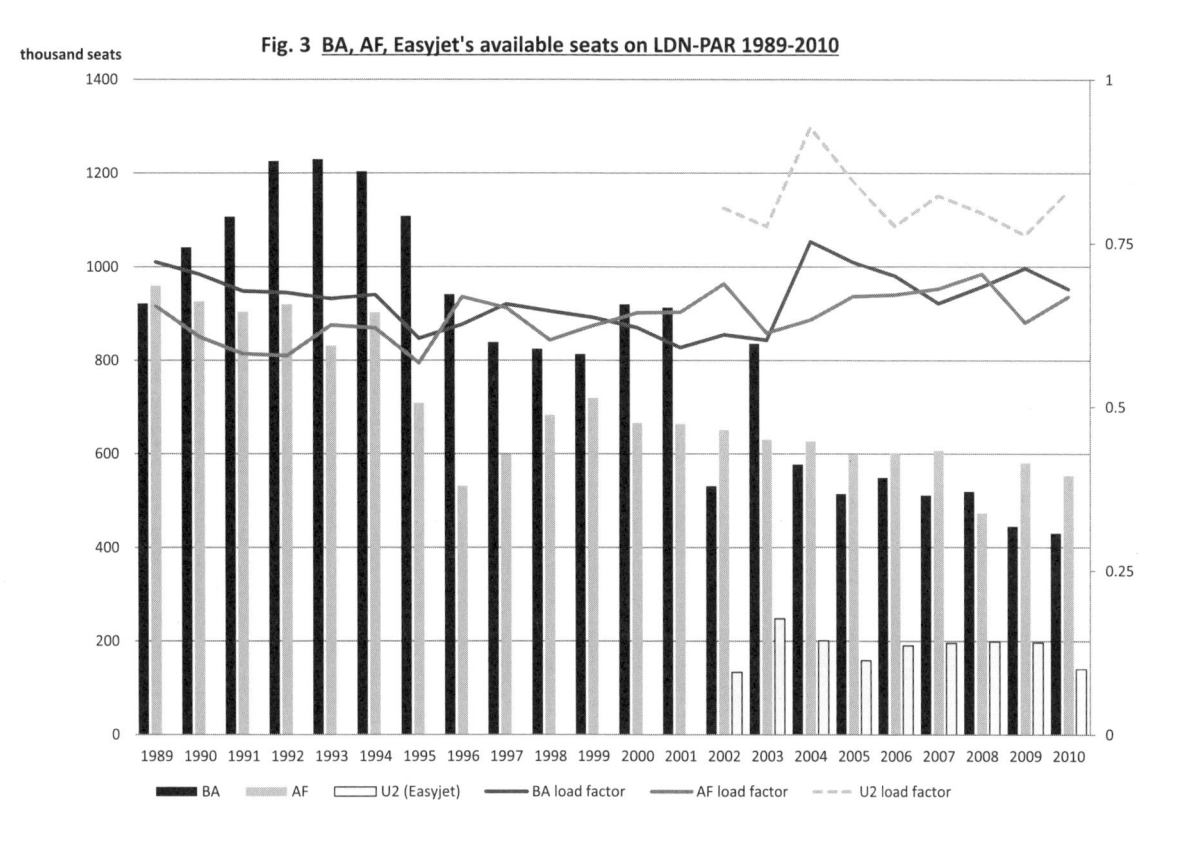

Fig. 3 BA, AF, Easyjet's available seats on LDN-PAR 1989-2010

ロンドン-フランクフルト路線

　Fig.4はロンドン-フランクフルト間で、90年代にはBA、LHともに一貫して座席数を拡大したが、2001～02年から縮小に転じた（LCCの運航状況は不明）。座席利用率をみると、90年代のBA（子会社ドイッチェBAを含むと思われる）は増席と座席利用率の低下が軌を一にし、2000年代にはその逆になっている[14]。しかし全般的にLHの座席利用率のほうが上回っており、近年ははっきりとBAよりも提供座席数および利用率の両方で上回る。この路線で仮にドイツ人旅客が多いならば、自国語で用が足りるという点で、機能的便益はLH便のほうが大きいだろう。LHは関係子会社ブリティッシュ・ミッドランド航空（BD）をこの路線に就航させず、自社運航に固執している。いっぽう路線網の関係でいえば、フランクフルトのハブ機能が高まったことにより、パリ路線のような陸運との競合はないが、BAからみたスポーク都市としての魅力は小さくなったと思われる。

ロンドン-アムステルダム路線

　ロンドン-アムステルダム間（Fig.5）はLCCイージージェットの成長過程が判然としている。97年に乗り入れを開始し、高座席利用率のまま急成長をとげ、旧来型の中小キャリアであるBDを代替したように見える。また既存キャリアにとって実質的な脅威になったのが2002年以降であることも見て取れる。BAの座席数推移をみると、93年から95年にかけて一時期減少したものの、2001年まで急速に伸ばしたのち、その後は50万席後半で落ち着いている。KLは90年代末と2000年代初頭に急伸しているが、子会社KLMuk（旧

---

(12) 同社のプレミアム旅客（ファーストクラスおよびビジネスクラス正規運賃負担客）の売上構成比は47.1％（08年3月期）にのぼり、他社にくらべ高水準と思われる。cf. "Registration Document of International Consolidated Airlines Group, S.A.", approved on Oct.26, 2010, p.70. また09年3月期の同社年次報告には"Global Premium Airline"がゴールとして掲げられ、A380型機ではエコノミークラス座席数を業界最低水準に設定する（Flight International, 19 Dec., 2012, "Analysis: BA loads A380s in favour of premium cabin", flightglobal.com）など、近年にいたり上層セグメントへの注力が明確である。

(13) オープンスカイズについては拙著pp.195-198。同社の運航実績は08年しかser.TFに報告されていない。なおワンワールドの米側パートナーであるアメリカン航空もNYC-PARを運航しているので、同社のプレミアムクラスと競合するはずだが、どのような分業が行われているかは不明である。

(14) ドイッチェBAについては拙著（2011）第7章第3節。

イノベーション・マネジメント研究

Fig. 4 BA, LH's available seats on LDN-FRA 1989-2010

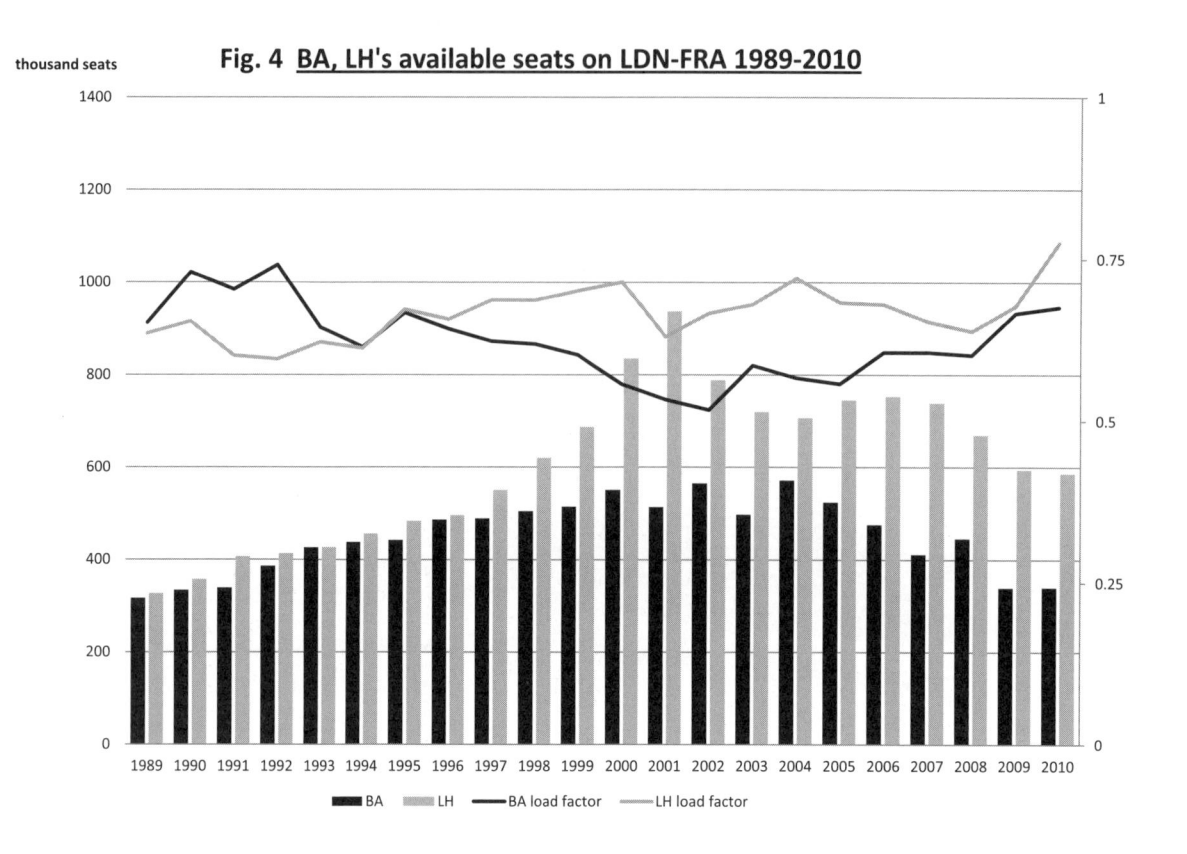

Fig. 5 BA, KL, British MIdland, and Easyjet's available seats on LDN-AMS 1989-2010

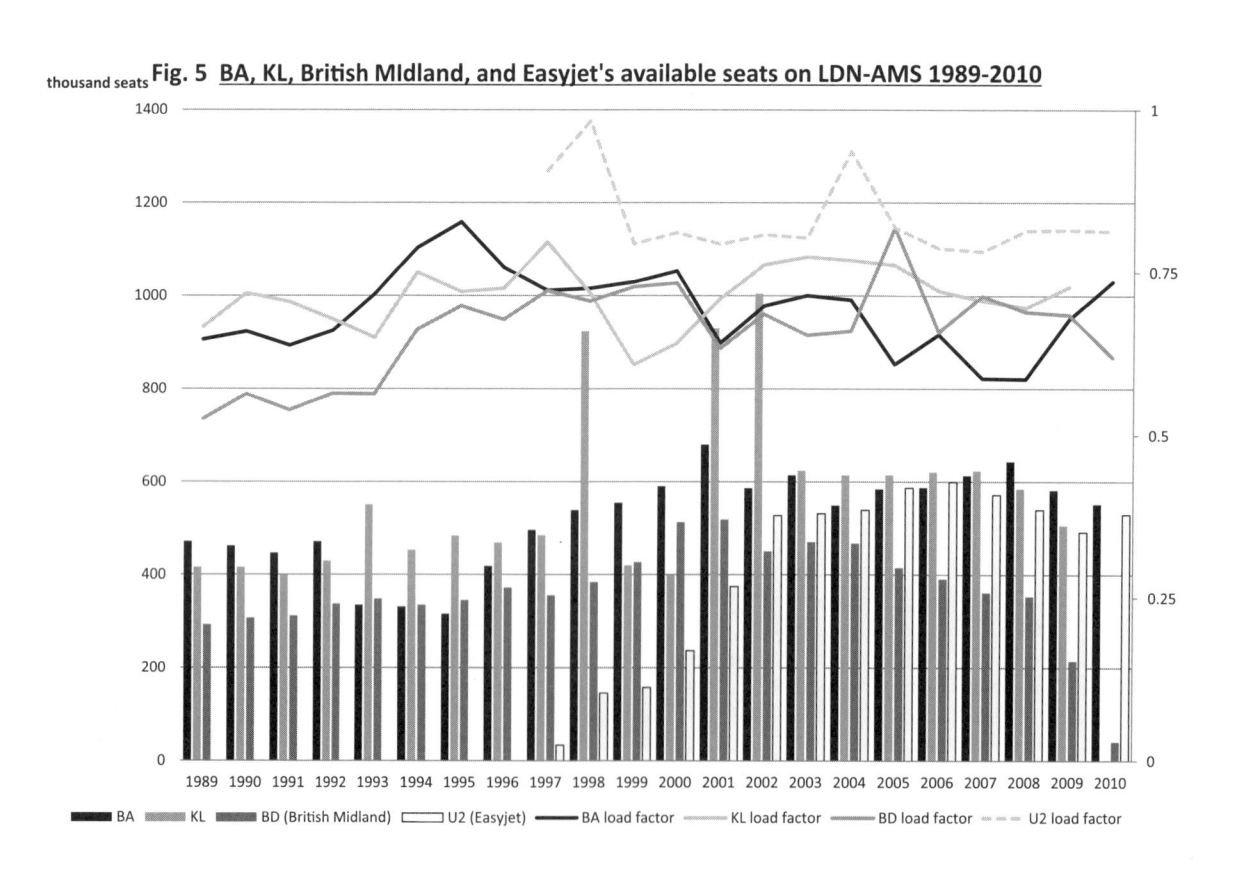

—38—

●研究ノート

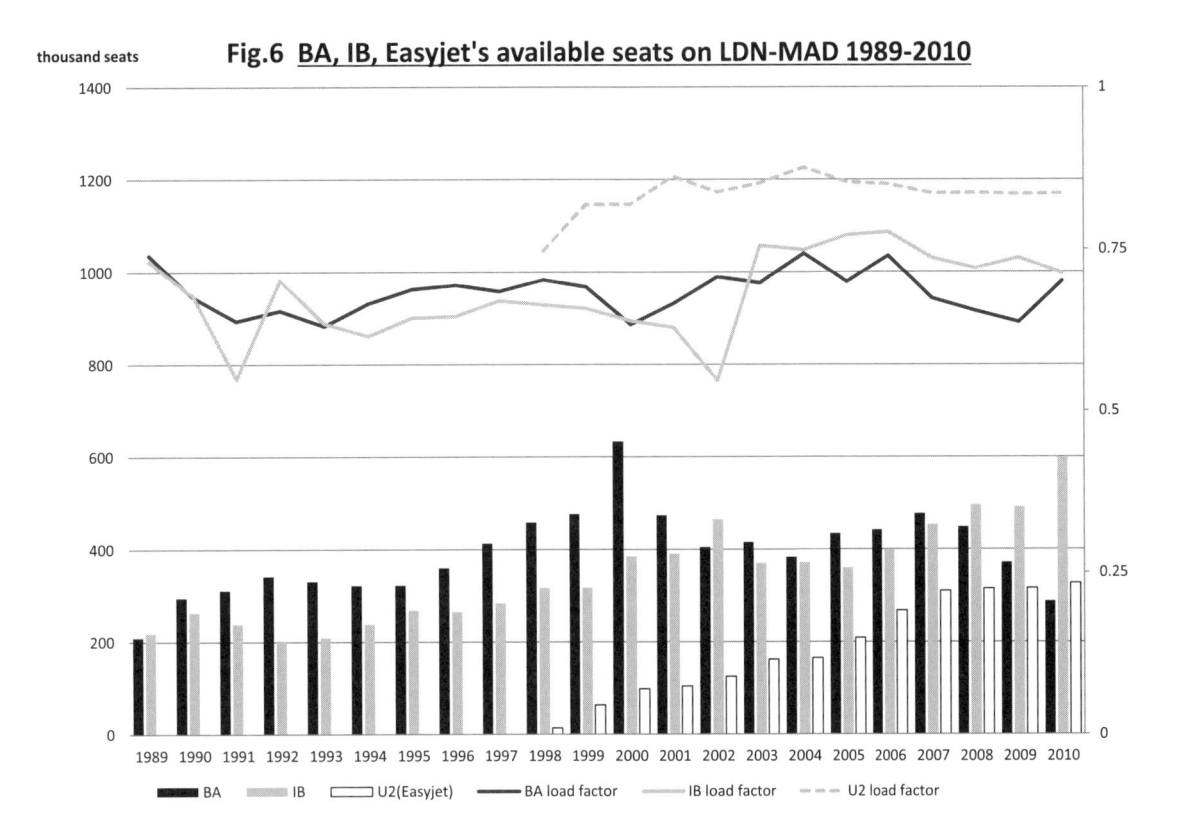

Fig.6 BA, IB, Easyjet's available seats on LDN-MAD 1989-2010

Air UK）のターボプロップ便が多く、BAやイージージェットを便数で圧倒しようと試みたのかもしれない。座席利用率は既存3社の差があまりないのに対し、やはりイージージェットは図抜けている。

アムステルダム路線は、LCCの挑戦にも拘わらず、かつ区間距離ではパリ並みの近さであるにも拘わらず、BAの上位路線では最も減少率が小さい。これはアライアンス相手を含む（すなわちKLコードによる）NYC-AMS路線の提供座席数および頻度が、BAのNYC-LON運航のほぼ半分、コードシェア分を除くと3分の1～4分の1程度にすぎないことが背景ではないかと思われる。つまり路線網の充実度においてBAはKLを凌ぐため[15]、アムステルダムはスポーク都市としてフランクフルトやパリよりも「おいしい」可能性がある。

ロンドン-マドリード路線

マドリード路線（Fig.6）はBAにとってアライアンス相手のハブを結ぶ路線で、アムステルダム路線の陰画とも言うべき様相になっている。BAがIBに出資を合意したのは98年、08年には最大株主になるとともに持ち合い関係に入り、経営統合の協議が開始された[16]。以降は明らかに当該路線をIBに委ねる形になっている。IBは対南米路線が充実しており、上述のアライアンスの契機にそぐう論理である。ロンドン-マドリード間の相対的重要度（国際線RPKに占める比率）はBAよりもIBのほうが大きく、この路線はIBが主に担当することで合意したと推定される。ただし両ハブ間の近さはLCCイージージェットの参入を招いており、とくにエコノミークラスの採算性は厳しいと思われる。

---

(15) 2010年の国際線運送量（RPK）でKLはBAの7割程度で、アメリカン航空よりさえも小さい。Cf. 野村宗訓編『新しい空港経営の可能性』関西学院大学出版会、2012、p.12. 2009年におけるロンドンからの対米便は3万2800便（うちBAが1万3300便）なのに対し、アムステルダムからのそれは1万便に満たず、うちKLは3300便にすぎない。なおKLがファーストクラスを撤廃したことも多少は関係があるかもしれないが、論証にはクラス別の座席利用率（不明）が必要だ。
(16) 経緯については拙著第11章第2節。

4. ポジションなきブランドからブランド志向のポジショニングへ

アムステルダム路線やマドリード路線は、LCCが既存大手の顧客を奪ったというよりも、新たな市場創造を行なったとする見解[17]を支持する例のようにも見える。LCCが圧倒的な低コスト低価格によるコモディティ化を促進したことは間違いないが、空の旅が旧西側諸国で「大衆化」したのはB747が登場して大量輸送時代の幕を開いた70年代である。規制緩和を率先した米国では80年代初頭にすでにアップスターツ（upstarts）が登場し、現在のLCCの祖型となっている[18]。ライアンエアがダブリン-ロンドン路線に初めて攻撃的な低価格を提示したのも1986年である。つまり「コモディティ化」は80年代から90年代にはヨーロッパで開始されており、かつ97年以降の域内航空運輸は斉一的に自由化されている。

それが2000年以降になると急展開した理由は何だろうか。ひとつには、2001年の世界同時テロとITバブル崩壊が、規制緩和の機運のなかで拡大策をとっていた既存大手を痛撃し、LCCがその隙間を縫う形で成長した点が挙げられる。もうひとつ見逃せないのが02年のユーロ一般流通開始で、域内運航に関する為替リスクを解消した点が大きい。逆に言えば、90年代までは既存大手が積極的に拡大していたのであり、それはLCCセグメントの取り込みを試みるものだった[19]。各社ヨーロッパ路線の提供座席数の増減はその間の事情を反映している。別の言い方をすると、既存大手は旧来のブランドのまま、低価格セグメントの取り込みを図り、自らブランドを侵食していたと考えられるが、それはなぜだろうか。

規制緩和以前のフラッグキャリアは、ブランド威力こそ強力だったが、その源泉は国際性、すなわち外国旅行という贅沢品をほぼ独占的に供給する点にあった。つまり国際路線を運航することだけでブランドを確保できたのであり、ポジションに腐心する必要はなかった。相手国キャリアとはバミューダ型の二国間協定のもと、便数（席数）・運賃ともに合意し、さらに収入プール契約を結んでいたからである。この点では、相手国キャリアは現在のアライアンス相手とほとんど変わらず、彼我のあいだに差別化を図る必要はなかったとさえ言えるかもしれない[20]。こうした状況でのブランド育成手段は新型機の導入と、新たな乗り入れ先の拡大と、新たな客層の取り込みだった[21]。換言すれば、「フォア・ザ・マーケット」の権益を占取していたことで、ブランド源泉は基本のKFS（Key Success Factors）だけで足りたのである。

BAのばあいでいうと、91年3月期年次報告書の冒頭に掲げられた企業目標（"Our goals"）の第4項目、"Service and Value: To provide overall superior service and good value for money in every market segment in which we compete"、がそれにあたる。"good value for money"は明確に低価格セグメントを含む文言だ。

90年代の既存大手はまだポジションが不明確で、フルライン・フルセグメント型の運航を行なっていた。フルラインとはすなわち短距離・長距離の路線ミックスであり、フルセグメントはプレミアムクラスからバジェット・トラベラーズまで全セグメントをカバーする政策である。上述の"Our goals"での文言、"every market segment in which we compete"は何ら争奪したいセグメントを特定していない。これは従来のフラッグキャリアにいわばポジションがなく、既得権益の占取によるブランドしかなかった時代の名残りではないだろうか。だが2000年代に入り、新しいビジネスモデルLCCが域内路線で躍進するにしたがい、破壊的イノベーションに直面した既存航空会社はほとんど初めて自社のポジションを考えねばならなく

---

(17) 篠辺修「アジアにおける航空競争の将来」、野村 op.cit., 第三章。
(18) ただし新型機を大量発注し運用を統一するLCCと違い、アップスターツの場合には中古機リースが主流だった。
(19) その意味では、「コモディティ化」を率先したのはLCCというより既存キャリア自身である。だがそれは既往のブランドを希釈することになったし、レベニュー・マネジメントによる価格政策の不透明さや財務上の困難もあって、「レガシー」のイメージを増幅する結果になったように思われる。
(20) 機内サービス内容さえもIATAで調整されていた。航空業界がもつ記号性の高さだけがブランド源泉だったともいえるかもしれない。中条（2012）の書名『航空幻想』もこの点に注目したものである。
(21) Cf. 拙稿「航空運輸業におけるブランド力」信州大学経済学論集46号（2002）、図7。また90年代に伸長したメガ・アライアンスに参加した各社が、当初ほぼ例外なく自社路線網（仮想的だが）の拡大を喧伝したのも、こうした従来の慣性が、少なくとも市場側にはあったことを意味する。なお、新型機の導入は今でもブランド源泉で、最近でもB787やA380がその例になっている。この点では、既存機種にフリートを統一せねばならないLCCは不利があるかもしれない。

なった。けだしポジショニングは他社（比較対象ないしライバル製品のポジション）があってこそ可能だからである。

　ポジショニングは当社製品やブランドの位置づけを指すが、転じてはターゲット顧客（誰に）を措定する作業でもある。さらに航空会社のばあいには、どの路線（どこに）も措定せねばならないだろう。しかし既存キャリアが仮にプレミアムクラスに特化すれば、大幅な規模縮小は避けられない。またビジネス旅客は利用する時間帯や曜日が集中するため、機材の運用効率も大幅に低下するだろう。いっぽう、LCCは機内アメニティが求められる長距離路線には就航しにくいビジネスモデルと思われ、まだ大陸間はフルサービス・フルセグメント運航が主流である。そこで長距離路線はフルセグメントのままとしながらも、短距離路線はプレミアムクラスの顧客基盤を確保できる程度まで減便し、いわば「生産調整」を行なう局面に至っていると思われる[22]。しかし短距離路線と大陸間（対米）路線の色分けをどうするか、またプレミアム旅客にどれだけ焦点を絞るかは、フラッグキャリア各社に温度差があるだろうし、LCCの展開にも左右されると思われる。各社とも模索中と思われるが、BAは上層セグメントへの「逃避」が最もはっきりとしている例かもしれない。

　以上が本ノートの結論だが、最後に今後を展望すると、路線では既存大手の長距離化とともに、アライアンス内での分業が進むだろう。しかし分業は路線間であって、座席クラス間での分業は困難ではないかと思われる。資本面での規制が緩和されれば、アライアンスよりも経営統合を選択する航空会社が増える可能性もある。それはLCCも同様で、LCCのビジネスモデルが可能なインフラが整えば、新興経済地域にも展開し、本稿でみたような既存大手の「生産調整」が起きるだろう。製品開発の面でいえば、既存キャリアの座席クラスではプレミアムクラスの高級化・差別化の追求による多様化が続く一方、エコノミークラスでは標準仕様が普及するのではないかと思われる[23]。
（2012年12月25日投稿、2013年1月22日受理）

---

[22] これは、既存キャリアの主な争奪対象がプレミアム旅客であり、全体の席数では十分な分析に至らないことを示唆する。ser. TFは座席クラス別のデータを提供しないので、今後の課題としたい。

[23] スター・アライアンスではすでに加盟各社に対しエコノミークラスの標準座席が提示されている。*Cf.* Aaron Karp, "Global Domination", *Air Transport World*, July 2012, *p.*30.

イノベーション・マネジメント研究

信州大学学生の環境とエネルギーに対する意識についての一考察

信州大学工学部環境機能工学科

教授　並木　光行

1. はじめに

　信州大学は、環境人材育成の先駆的な取り組みを行っている大学である。平成13（2001）年、工学部が国公立大学の学部・大学院として初めて、国際環境規格ISO14001の認証を取得した[1]。この工学部によるISO14001の認証取得を契機に、平成14（2002）年、大学本部は、「環境マインドプロジェクト推進本部会議」を設置し、更に平成16（2004）年、"環境マインドをもつ人材の養成とエコキャンパスの構築"を目指した全学的な活動を開始した。本活動は、環境関連の基礎・専門科目の教育を実施することは勿論、化学薬品、実験廃液、生協食堂の排水、ゴミ、省エネ等、キャンパス内の身近な環境を教材として、日々の地道な実体験を通し、環境マインドをもつ人材を育むものである[2]。これにより、信州大学は、いまや全国の環境教育の拠点のモデルとなり、「環境の信州大学」と呼ばれるようになっている[3]。

　ところで、平成23（2011）年3月11日（金）、東日本大震災及びそれに伴う東京電力福島第一原子力発電所の事故（以下「東電福島原発事故」という。）が発生した。原子力は安全であるという大前提が大きく揺らぎ、我が国の原子力発電に依存したエネルギー選択を白紙から見直さなければならなくなった。そして、最終的には、ひとりひとりが、今後の環境問題やエネルギー問題に対する選択が極めて広い意味での国の豊かさや在り方を決める国民的な選択であり、将来世代に影響の及ぶ課題の選択であることを再認識することとなった。

　このような背景のもと、政府のエネルギー・環境会議は、平成24（2012）年6月、今後のエネルギー選択についての国民的議論を開始するため、エネルギーと環境に関する3つのシナリオを用意した[4]。原発比率を震災前の2010年の実績値約26％から、2030年までに0％程度、あるいは15％程度、または20〜25％程度まで下げていくという3つのシナリオである。政府は、これら3つのシナリオについての7月、8月の国民的議論を踏まえた上で、今後のエネルギー選択及びそれと表裏一体の地球温暖化国内対策に関して責任を持って結論を出す、とした。そして、9月14日（金）、「2030年代に原発稼働ゼロを可能とするよう、グリーンエネルギーを中心にあらゆる政策資源を投入」するとした、『革新的エネルギー・環境戦略』[5]を決定することとなった。

　本稿は、環境人材育成について先駆的な取り組みを行う信州大学の学生が、東日本大震災及びそれに伴う東電福島原発事故後、環境とエネルギーに対して、どのような意識を持っていたのか、また、エネルギー・環境会議の用意したエネルギーと環境に関する3つのシナリオについて、7月、8月の国民的議論の実施期間中、どのような意見を持っていたのか、について分析したものである。そして、本分析に基づき、今後の信州大学におけ

---

(1) 信州大学工学部創立60周年記念事業実行委員会（編）（2010）信州大学工学部　創立60年のあゆみ．信州大学工学部・信州大学工学部同窓会，50．
(2) 信州大学（2006）環境報告書2006－いのちのつながりのために－．信州大学環境報告書，6．
(3) 並木光行（2012）信州大学若里キャンパスにおける環境人材育成への取組み－グリーンMOT教育プログラムとGMPとの連携についての一考察－．第2回環境人材育成研究交流大会発表要旨，12．
(4) エネルギー・環境会議（2012）エネルギー・環境に関する選択肢．エネルギー・環境会議決定．
(5) エネルギー・環境会議（2012）革新的エネルギー・環境戦略．エネルギー・環境会議決定．

●調査報告

表1　調査票

（1）　あなたが、最も身近に感じる環境問題は何か、その理由と解決策の案を示しながらひとつあげ、500字程度で述べよ。
　　　なお、環境問題の中身や、その問題の大小等は問わない。

（2）　あなたが、国際的に重要と考える環境問題は何か、また、国内的に重要と考える環境問題は何か、について、その理由と解決策の案を示しながらひとつづつあげ、500字程度で述べよ。

（3）　政府のエネルギー・環境会議は、エネルギーと環境に関する3つのシナリオを用意して、この3つのシナリオに関して国民的議論を開始し、その上で、今後のエネルギー選択、それと表裏一体の地球温暖化国内対策に関する方針を出すこととしている。
　　　3つのシナリオとは、電力量における原発比率を震災前の2010年の実績値約26％から、2030年までに0％程度、あるいは15％程度、または20～25％程度まで下げていくという3つのシナリオである。
　　　この3つのシナリオのうち、あなたはどのシナリオを選択するのが適切であると考えるか、理由を付して1000字程度で述べよ。理由には、主に環境保護の観点からの理由を含めること。また、理由は、適切な用語を用いた論理的なものであること。
　　　なお、理由には、以下の用語等を用いること。
　　　・持続可能な社会の構築（持続可能性、環境と両立する社会等、同様の意味の用語等を含む）
　　　・原発の安全確保（原子力災害、原発事故、放射能汚染等、同様の意味の用語等を含む）
　　　・エネルギー安定供給（エネルギー安全保障、エネルギー確保等、同様の意味の用語等を含む）
　　　・地球温暖化防止（CO_2削減、気温上昇の緩和等、同様の意味の用語等を含む）
　　　・コスト（環境と経済の両立、グリーン経済、景気への配慮等、同様の意味の用語等を含む）

注）学部1年生には（3）の設問のみを、500字程度で述べるよう、質問した。

る、「環境マインドを持つ人材の育成」のための教育プログラムの更なる発展等に向けた一考察を行うものである。

2. 方法

平成24年8月、信州大学工学部3年生[注1]（環境政策概論を履修した電気電子工学科、土木工学科、建築学科、物質工学科、情報工学科、環境機能工学科の6学科の学生）37名（男性86.5％、女性13.5％、有効回答者数32名、有効回収率83.8％）及び、信州大学理科系学部1年生[注2]（グリーンテクノロジーを履修した理学部、医学部、工学部、農学部、繊維学部の5学部の学生）58名（男性91.4％、女性8.6％、有効回答者数46名、有効回収率79.3％）を対象に、授業時間内に自由回答の質問形式で環境とエネルギーに対する意識を調査した（表1）。

なお、設問（3）において用いるように示した5つの用語等（以下、「5つの用語等」と略す）は、『エネルギー・環境に関する選択肢』[6]で、エネルギーの選択を行うに当たって考慮すべき重要な4つの視点として挙げられた1）原子力の安全確保と将来リスクの低減、2）エネルギー安全保障の強化、3）地球温暖化問題解決への貢献、4）コストの抑制と空洞化防止、に環境政策上必須の概念である5）持続可能な社会の構築、を加えて作成したものである。

3. 結果

(1) 最も身近に感じる環境問題

工学部3年生の約1/4は、「ゴミ問題（廃棄物の発生量増加、不適正な処理等。以下、同様）」を最も身近に感じる環境問題であるとしていた。東日本大震災及びそれに伴う東電福島原発事故により関連していると思われる、「エネルギー安定供給（原子力を始めとしたエネルギーの確保、安全保障等。以下、同様）」、「原発の安全確保（原子力災害の防止、放射能汚染対策等。以下、同様）」についての回答もみられた。「地球温暖化防止」については、「ゴミ問題」に次いで、最も身近に感じる環境問題であるとされていた（図1）。

(2) 国際的に重要と考える環境問題

工学部3年生の半数以上が、「地球温暖化防止」を国際的に重要と考える環境問題であるとしていた。次いで「エネルギー安定供給」が多く、それ

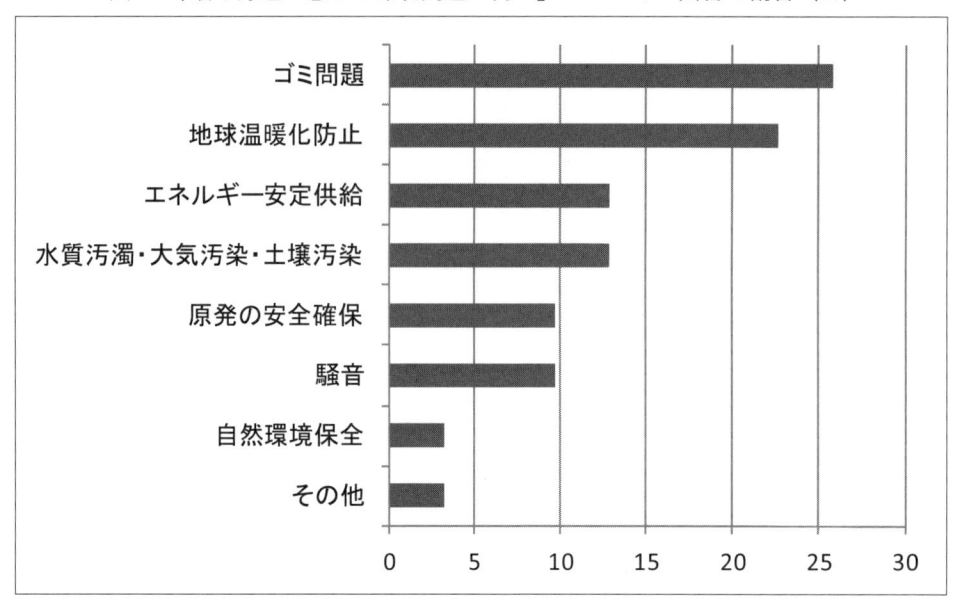

図1 「最も身近に感じる環境問題は何か」についての回答の割合（%）

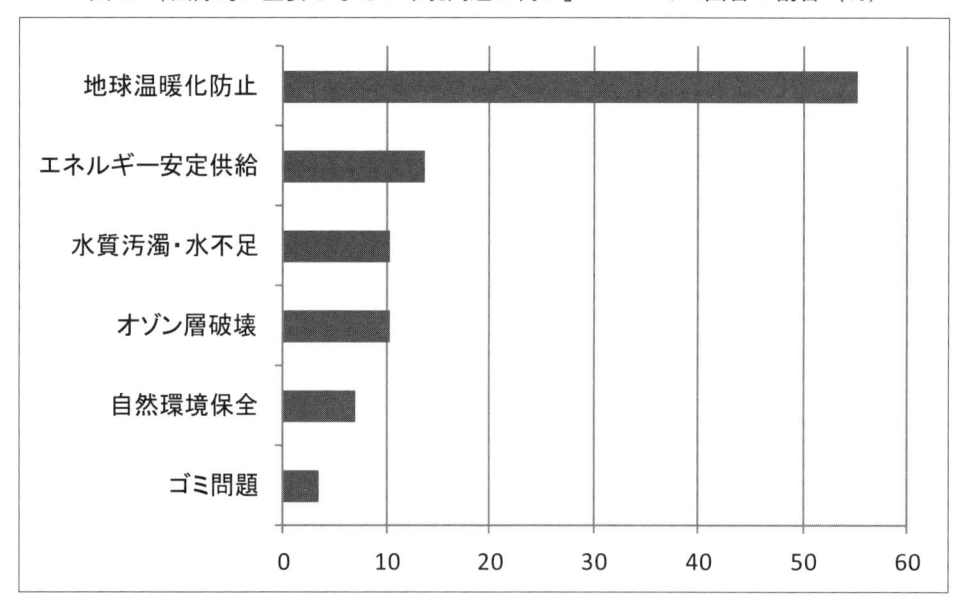

- ゴミ問題
- 地球温暖化防止
- エネルギー安定供給
- 水質汚濁・大気汚染・土壌汚染
- 原発の安全確保
- 騒音
- 自然環境保全
- その他

図2 「国際的に重要と考える環境問題は何か」についての回答の割合（%）

- 地球温暖化防止
- エネルギー安定供給
- 水質汚濁・水不足
- オゾン層破壊
- 自然環境保全
- ゴミ問題

以外には「自然環境保全」等の回答もみられたが、いずれも比較的少数の意見であった（図2）。

(3) 国内的に重要と考える環境問題

工学部3年生の約1/3が、「原発の安全確保」及び「地球温暖化防止」をそれぞれ国内的に重要と考える環境問題であるとしていた。次いで、「ゴミ問題」や「エネルギー安定供給」についての回答が多く、それ以外は比較的少数であった（図3）。

(4) 今後のエネルギー選択についてのシナリオ

エネルギー・環境会議が示した、エネルギーと環境に関する3つのシナリオにおける原発比率に対する回答は、工学部3年生、学部1年生ともに同様の傾向を示し、「原発比率15％」（以下、「15％」と略す）を選択した者が1/2以上、「原発比率0％」（以下、「0％」と略す）及び「原発比率20〜25％」（以下、「20〜25％」と略す）を選択した者が、それぞれ1/5程度となっていた（図4）。

20代の全国平均の回答は、0％に賛成が50.3％、15％に強く賛成が44.9％、20〜25％に強く賛成が28.2％であった[7]のと比較する[注3]と、信州大学の学生においては、0％の割合が低かったと言える。

図5に、工学部3年生について、原発比率に対する回答と、設問(1)「最も身近に感じる環境問

●調査報告

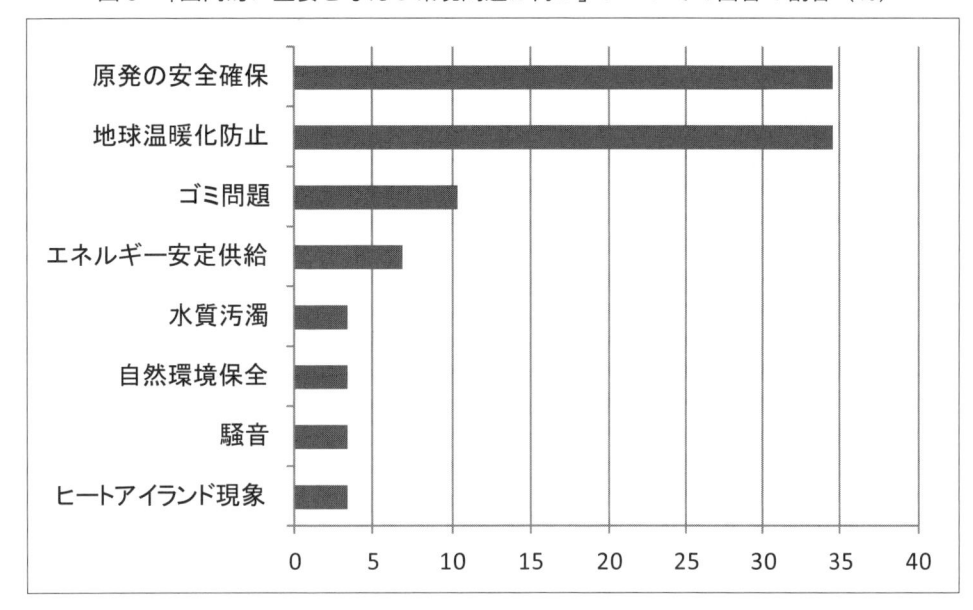

図3 「国内的に重要と考える環境問題は何か」についての回答の割合（％）

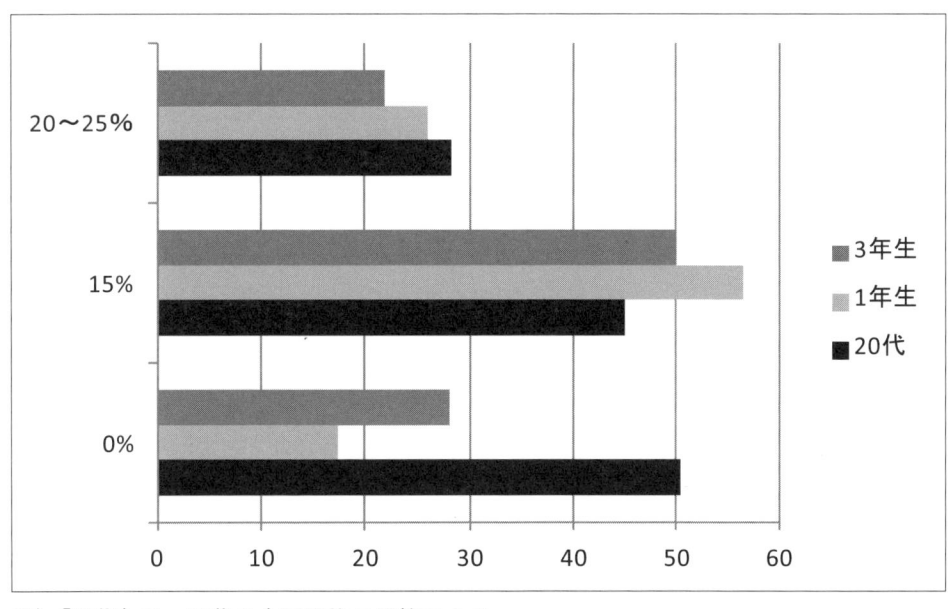

- 原発の安全確保
- 地球温暖化防止
- ゴミ問題
- エネルギー安定供給
- 水質汚濁
- 自然環境保全
- 騒音
- ヒートアイランド現象

図4 3つのシナリオにおける原発比率に対する回答の割合（％）

- 20～25%
- 15%
- 0%

凡例：3年生、1年生、20代

注）「20代」は、20代の全国平均の回答である。

題は何か」及び設問（2）「国際的に重要と考える環境問題は何か、また、国内的に重要と考える環境問題は何か」の回答との関係を示す。

まず、0％を選択した者は、「エネルギー安定供給」を身近に感じる環境問題、国際的に重要な環境問題、国内的に重要な環境問題（以下、「身近・国際・国内の環境問題」と略す）の何れにも挙げていなかった。「エネルギー安定供給」を身近・国際・国内の環境問題として挙げた者の割合は、15％、20～25％の順に増加していた。

また、0％を選択した者より、15％や20～25％を選択した者の方が、「原発の安全確保」を身近・国際・国内の環境問題として挙げた割合が高かった。

一方で、「地球温暖化防止」を身近・国際・国内の環境問題として挙げた者の割合は、0％及び

(7) エネルギー・環境の選択肢に関する討論型世論調査実行委員会（2012）エネルギー・環境の選択肢に関する討論型世論調査 調査報告書, 19-21.

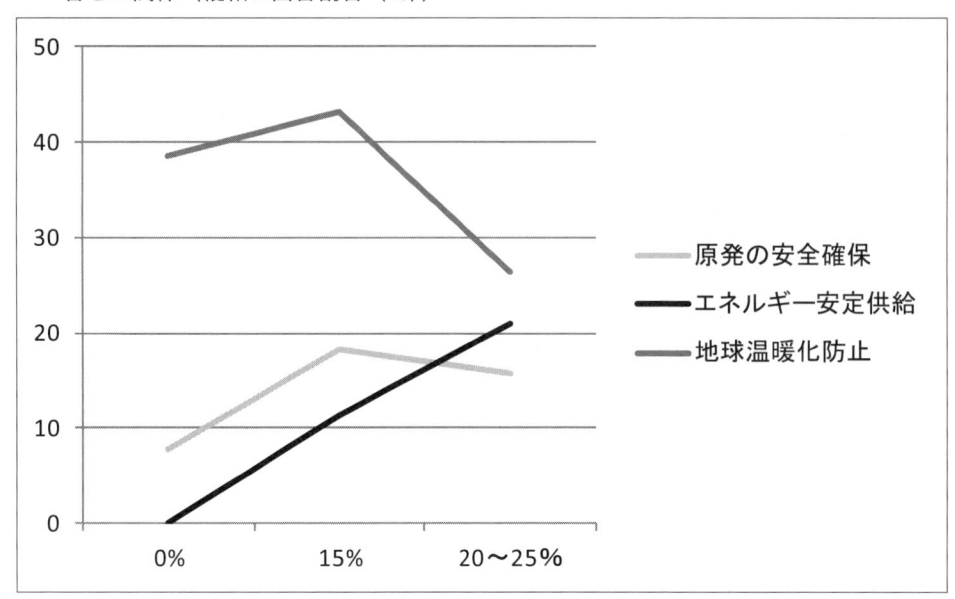

図5　3つのシナリオにおける原発比率に対する回答と、設問（1）及び設問（2）の回答との関係（縦軸は回答割合（%））

表2　判断基準の優先順位（20代の全国平均）

1番目に重視すること　原発の安全確保（63.9%）
2番目に重視すること　エネルギー安定供給（42.0%）
3番目に重視すること　地球温暖化防止（31.8%）

注）括弧内は回答者の割合
出典；エネルギー・環境の選択肢に関する討論型世論調査　調査報告書をもとに著者作成

15%では4割前後でほぼ等しかったのに対し、20～25%では2.5割程度まで減少していた。

表2に、原発比率の判断基準の優先項目についての回答（20代の全国平均）を示す。判断基準の優先項目は、「原発の安全確保」、「エネルギー安定供給」、「地球温暖化防止」の順になっていた。

更に、工学部3年生及び学部1年生について、3つのシナリオにおける原発比率に対する回答と、5つの用語等との関係を図6～8に示した。なお、図6～8の縦軸は、「持続可能な社会の構築」、「原発の安全確保」、「エネルギー安定供給」、「地球温暖化防止」、「コスト」の5つの用語等ごとに、それを、それぞれの原発比率を選択する積極的理由として捉えた[注4]者の割合（%）を示している。

0%、15%、20～25%のいずれについても、工学部3年生と学部1年生とで、5つの用語等を積極的理由として捉えた者の割合に有意差はない（p>0.05、Mann-Whitney検定）。

そして、図6～8を比較した場合、工学部3年生、学部1年生ともに、「原発の安全確保」を積極的理由とする者の割合は、0%、15%、20～25%を選択した者の順に減少傾向にあり、「エネルギー安定供給」及び「地球温暖化防止」については、それを積極的理由とする者の割合は、0%、15%、20～25%を選択した者の順におおむね増加傾向にあった。

4. 考察

工学部3年生は、信州大学において、既に「環境マインドを持つ人材の育成」のための教育プログラムを受けてきている学生である。一方、学部1年生は、これから本格的に、「環境マインドを持つ人材の育成」のための教育プログラムが始まって行く学生たちである。これを前提に、以下、調査結果を分析して行きたい。

全国調査[8]では、学生が最も関心を持っている環境問題は「地球環境問題」であった[注5]が、工学部3年生には、身近に感じる環境問題として「ゴミ問題」を挙げる者の割合が高かった。これは、大学生となり、親元を離れ一人暮らしを始めた学生[注6]が、自己の生活に起因するゴミの量があまりに多いことや、その出し方等が適切に行われてい

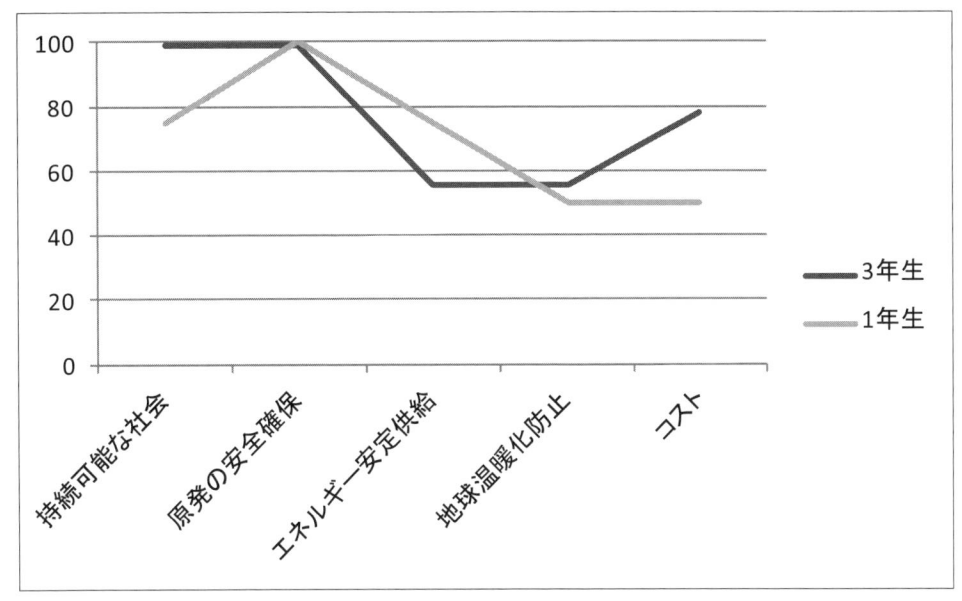

図6　原発比率0％を選択した者における5つの用語等の関係（縦軸は割合（％））

注）「持続可能な社会の構築」は「持続可能な社会」と表記している（以下、同様）。

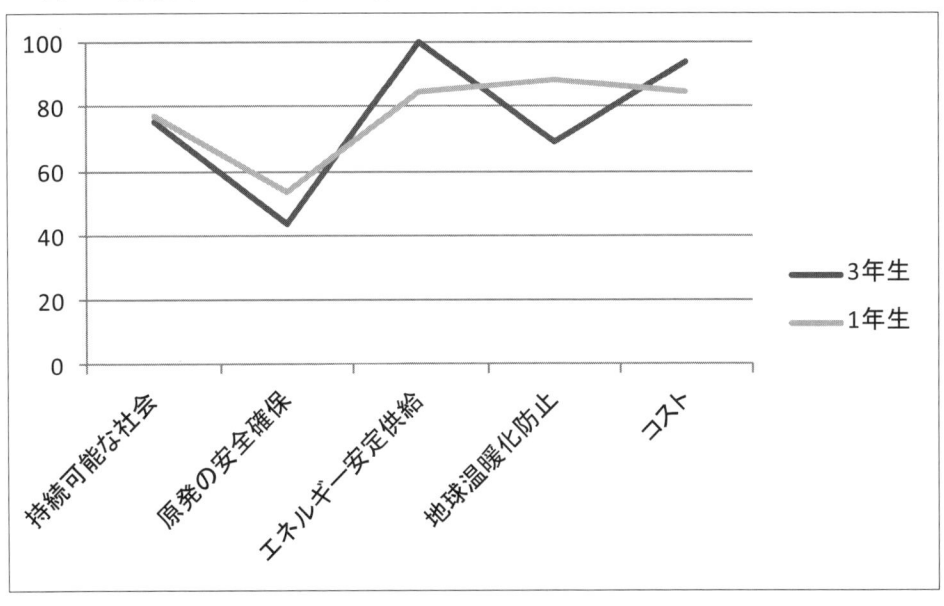

図7　原発比率15％を選択した者における5つの用語等の関係（縦軸は割合（％））

ないことを知った（いわゆる一般廃棄物についての知識を深めたこと）のに加え、信州大学におけるエコキャンパス構築活動の中で、実際に大学で発生する大量のゴミを処理等しているため（いわゆる産業廃棄物についての知識を深めたため）であろう。

但し、「地球温暖化防止」についても、身近・国際・国内の環境問題として、それを挙げる者の割合は高かった。平成22（2010）年の信州大学大学院生、学部1年生を対象とした調査[9]においても、「地球温暖化防止」を深刻であると回答した者の割合は高く、基本的に、学生の「地球温暖化

---

(8) 環境省総合環境政策局環境計画課（2011）環境にやさしいライフスタイル実態調査平成22年度調査報告書，90-97．
(9) 柳町晴美（2010）大学生の環境マインドに関する日本と中国の比較調査－信州大学における調査概要－．信州大学「グリーンMOT（技術経営）教育プログラムの推進」事業報告書，45-55．

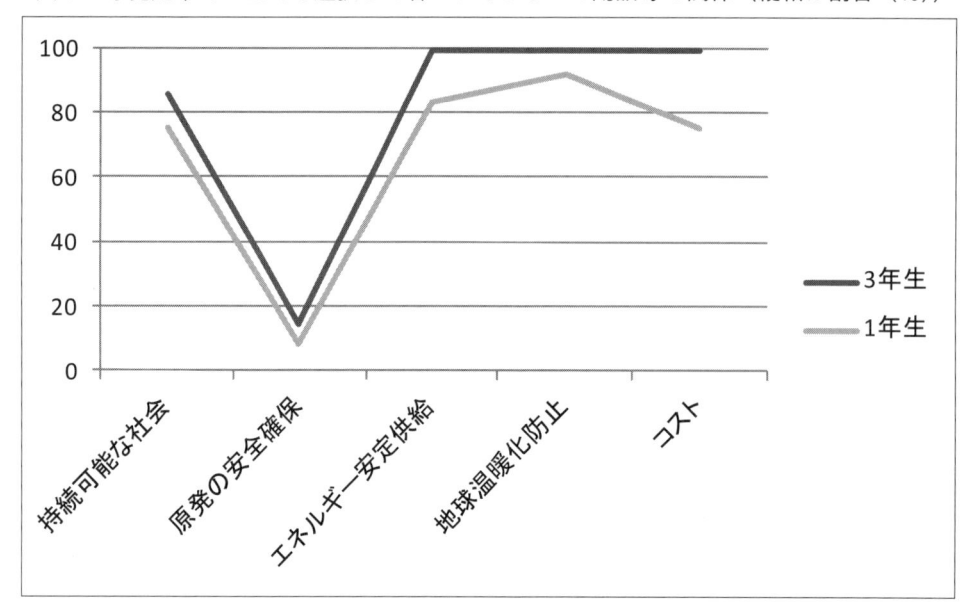

図8　原発比率20〜25％を選択した者における5つの用語等の関係（縦軸は割合（％））

「防止」を重要な環境問題と考える認識には、大きな変化はないものと思われた[注7]。

「原発の安全確保」については、国内的に重要な環境問題として挙げる者は多くいたが、最も身近に感じる環境問題として挙げた者は少数で、実感を持っている者は少ないことが理解できた。これは、長野県においては、東日本大震災や東電福島原発事故の被害を、報道により知ることはできても、直接には実感することはできず、また、大学での授業や実習においても、これらを取り上げたものが少ないからであろう。

一方、同じく東日本大震災や東電福島原発事故に関連すると思われる「エネルギー安定供給」については、身近・国際・国内の環境問題の何れにおいても、一定程度の割合で挙げる者が存在していた。電力やガソリン等のエネルギーについての問題は、エネルギー自体が日常使用するものでもあり、長野県で生活していても、直接にその存在等を認識することができるからであろう。

その他の「自然環境保全」等については、上記の「ゴミ問題」、「地球温暖化防止」、「原発の安全確保」、「エネルギー安定供給」と比較すると、身近・国際・国内の環境問題の何れにおいても、挙げる者の割合は比較的少数であった。これも、先の平成22（2010）年の結果と同様の傾向である。

次に、以上の身近・国際・国内の環境問題と、エネルギーと環境に関する3つのシナリオにおける原発比率に対する回答との関係についてみると、0％、15％、20〜25％を選択した者の順に、身近・国際・国内の環境問題として「エネルギー安定供給」を挙げた者の割合が増加していた。こ

れは、より安定したエネルギーの供給等を求めた学生たちが、そのためには、より高い原発比率が必要と考えたからであろうと思われた。それどころか、むしろ、より安定したエネルギーの供給等を求めることが、原発比率として、0％、15％、20〜25％のそれぞれを選択することの最大の要因となったのではないかとも考えられた。なぜなら、原発比率を選択するに際し、「地球温暖化防止」を最重要視した場合、身近・国際・国内の環境問題としてそれを挙げる者の割合は0％、15％、20〜25％を選択した者の順に増加するだろうと思われるが、そうはなっておらず、また、「原発の安全確保」を最重要視した場合、それを挙げる者の割合は0％、15％、20〜25％を選択した者の順に減少すると思われるが、そうもなっていないからである。なお、図6〜8を比較した場合、工学部3年生では、「原発の安全確保」を積極的理由とした者の割合は、0％、15％、20〜25％を選択した者の順に減少傾向にあり、また、「エネルギー安定供給」及び「地球温暖化防止」を積極的理由とした者の割合は、0％、15％、20〜25％を選択した者の順に増加傾向にあった。これは、工学部3年生が「原発の安全確保」や「地球温暖化防止」についても、最重要視はしていないが、原発比率を選択する上での要素の一つとしては考慮していたことを示していると思われる。

一方、『エネルギー・環境の選択肢に関する討論型世論調査 調査報告書』では、原発比率を選択する上での判断基準の第1位は「原発の安全確保」となっていた（20代の全国平均）。原発比率に対する回答そのものについても、信州大学の学

生では、20代の全国平均と比較して0%の割合が低かった。これらもやはり、信州大学の学生が「原発の安全確保」について実感を持っていないことがその理由となっていると思われる。

更に、工学部3年生と学部1年生とでは、原発比率の選択に対する回答の割合や、5つの用語等を積極的理由として捉えた者の割合において、大きな差は見られなかった。今回の原子力災害についての知識は、平成23（2011）年3月11日（金）以前には、ほぼ完全に環境問題としては想定さえされておらず、大学においても、知識として教育されることは殆どなかったであろう。この意味で、工学部3年生と学部1年生とでは、原子力災害についての知識に大きな違いはなく、それを踏まえた原発比率の選択に対する考え方にも大きな差が出ることがなかったのではなかろうか。

以上より、今後の信州大学における「環境マインドを持つ人材の育成」のための教育プログラムにおいては、本稿での学生の「ごみ問題」に対する考え方等を踏まえた場合には、既存の環境問題やエネルギー問題に対する知識や考え方を与えるような教育プログラムを引き続き実施して行くことはもちろん重要であるが、しかし、一方で、原子力災害に対する判断についての結果等を踏まえると、原子力災害のような、ある意味、想定外の環境問題やエネルギー問題にも十分対応できる、環境とエネルギーに対する総合的な分析力を身に付けさせるための教育を実施して行く必要もあるのではなかろうかと考えられた。

（2012年12月18日投稿、12月27日受理）

注
- 注1 「1. はじめに」に記載したとおり、信州大学では環境マインド教育を実施している。「環境政策概論」は、工学部3年生を対象とした環境マインド教育のための学部共通科目（選択科目の一つ）である。なお、信州大学HP（http://www.shinshu-u.ac.jp/）によれば、平成24年度の工学部3年生の学生数は約640名となっている。
- 注2 全学の1年生にとって、環境マインドに関する科目（環境関連科目）は必修科目であり、複数開講されている環境関連科目から最低1科目を履修しなければならない。「グリーンテクノロジー」は、理科系学生向けの環境関連科目に該当している。なお、信州大学HP（http://www.shinshu-u.ac.jp/）によれば、平成24年度の理科系学部1年生は約1600名となっている。
- 注3 『エネルギー・環境の選択肢に関する討論型世論調査』では、0％、15％、20〜25％のそれぞれについて、「強く反対する」を0、「強く賛成する」を10、「ちょうど中間」を5とした10の尺度から1つの尺度を選ぶことを求め、尺度6-10の合計を、それぞれの賛成意見としている。
- 注4 「積極的理由として捉えた」とは、用いることとされた用語等を、（1）その原発比率を選択した理由として使用し、かつ、（2）理由においても「AではあるがBのため」等のAのような逆接的な使用はしなかったことを意味している。
- 注5 「環境にやさしいライフスタイル実態調査」において関心のある環境問題として「地球温暖化」を挙げた者は62.9％であったのに対し、「廃棄物などの発生量増加」、「不法投棄など廃棄物の不適正な処理」を挙げた者は、それぞれ21.0％、24.2％（合計で45.2％）となっていた。
- 注6 信州大学HP（http://www.shinshu-u.ac.jp/campus_life/）によれば、信州大学学生の約7割は長野県外の出身者である。
- 注7 平成22（2010）年当時の学部1年生は、平成24（2012）年現在の3年生である。

イノベーション・マネジメント専攻での教育体験に対する修了生の意識調査　結果報告

信州大学経営大学院

教授　今村　英明
助手　髙相　栄美

1. 調査の目的

2012年は、本専攻創設10周年にあたる。これを一つの節目と捉え、これまでの修了生が本専攻で受けた教育体験や教育内容に対して、現時点で感じている認識や満足度、改善のための意見や提言などを調査し、本専攻の今後の教育を改善していくための一つの参考材料とすることが目的である。

調査の主な項目としては、入学時の目的とその達成度、入学前の期待と実際の体験とのギャップ、本専攻での教育体験で修了後役立っていること、印象に残る科目・教員、本専攻での教育への時間・金銭「投資」の価値、本専攻への不満・課題認識・感想・提言などである。

2. 調査の方法

2012年6月調査の実施に関し所属機関の承認を得た。それに基づき下記の内容にて調査を行なった。
(ア) 実施時期：　2012年7月1日〜8月1日
(イ) 調査対象：　その時点で本専攻を修了した82名[1]
(ウ) 方　　法：　記名・記述式アンケート調査（調査票は末尾添付）
(エ) 実施経路：　電子メールもしくは郵送で、告知・依頼・回収
(オ) 回収状況：　82名中36名。回収率44％
(カ) 結果処理：　2012年9月の専攻会議にて、調査票の集計表を配布した。さらに同年12月の本専攻アドバイザリー会議で報告した[2]。

3. 調査結果の要旨

(ア) 回答状況：
　　修了生82名に対して、36名（44％）からの回答であった。過半数には達していないが、記名・記述式のアンケートとしては比較的回答率は高かった[3]。
(イ) 入学時の目的とその達成度：
　　修了生の入学時の目的意識は多様である。多かったのは、全般的な経営スキル向上、自社・自組織経営の方向性模索、具体的なテーマ研究などである。一方で、キャリアや生き方を探索するような漠然とした目的意識の学生も混在していた。またイノベーションや起業を目的として前面に打ち出していた回答は意外に少なかった。

　　3人に2人（66％）が、「入学目的を達成した」と認識している。残る約3分の一の「未達成」回答の理由の大半は、入学後のテーマ変更、修了後の業務・処遇などいわば本人に起因するものであった。
(ウ) 入学前の認識と入学後の認識とのギャップ：
　　42％が「ギャップ大」と回答している。「ギャップなし」との回答は28％であった。「ギャップ大」という回答の3分の2は、「期待よりもよかった」という認識である。逆

---

(1) その時点で修了した86名の内、連絡先不明者や物故者など4名を除いた。
(2) アドバイザリー会議の討議内容などは、別途報告書等が作成される予定である。
(3) なお記名・記述式により、回答が偏った可能性はあり得る。但し、その偏向度は推定できない。また修了年次毎にアンケート回答率と肯定的回答率との関係を分析したが有意な相関は認められなかった。

に「期待外れ」の理由（3件）は、期待したプログラムの欠如・不足や非実業出身者へのケア不足などを挙げている。
（エ）修了後、役立っていること：
　　回答が比較的多かったものとしては、①客観性・論理性・仮説思考など、思考法・問題へのアプローチに関する学び、②教員・同級生・修了生との交流・ネットワーク、③特定課題研究の厳しい指導、論文の達成感、またそれらを通じた人間的な成長、自信、ガッツなどであった。
（オ）受講して良かった科目：
　　創設初期は、経営戦略論、経営組織論などの基本科目、工学系や専門性の高い科目などである。また体制整備途上でもあり、外部講師への評価も高い。近年は、マーケティング、ロジカルプレゼンテーションなどへの好評価が加わる。逆に、外部講師や工学系科目への印象は相対的に後退している。本専攻の看板であるはずの「イノベーション概論」「プロジェクト演習」「特定課題研究指導」「グリーンＭＯＴ」などへの言及は意外に少ない。
（カ）残念・不満だったこと：
　　働きながら学ぶ社会人学生が多いため、開講時間・時期の問題指摘が最も多い。また専攻開設初期の体制不備への不満も強い（その指摘の多くは、現在はかなり改善されているが）。教育内容・質、教員・サポート体制などの不満は、現在改善されたもの、依然課題となっている部分が存在（例：海外企業視察などの中断など）。
（キ）本専攻での時間・金銭投資と教育経験の価値が見合っているか、の評価：
　　全体の72％が「時間・金銭投資に見合う価値があった」と回答している。「見合う」と判断した理由は、人脈・交流、自分の成長、コスト・パフォーマンス、プログラムの中身の濃さなどである。一方、「見合わない」（2名）との判断理由は、学費負担の重さ、一部教育内容の問題などである。「分からない」「その他」の判断理由は、判断するには時期尚早、ジョイント・ディグリーで本専攻での投資の負担感がない、などである。
（ク）感想・意見・提言：
　　多数の自由記述のコメントを頂いた。プログラムの内容・質の改善への提言、修了後の継続学習や交流への期待・提言・要望、本専攻の社会的な知名度向上への期待・提言が多かった。また本専攻での体験の感想とともに、本専攻への感謝と声援も頂いた

4. 調査結果からの示唆

（ア）本専攻での教育体験への満足度は、入学時の目的の達成度、入学時の期待との合致度、時間・金銭投資へのリターンなどの物差しで見る限り、概ね3分の2程度で、「70点」「まずまずの評価」と言える。
（イ）開設初期2〜3年間の体制未整備により、当事者の努力にも関わらず、学生に不便や不満を感じさせた部分があったことは、率直に反省し、またお詫びしなければならない。一方、初期も含めこの間、プログラムを支えて頂いた他学部・外部の諸先生方には、改めて深く御礼申し上げねばならない。
（ウ）その後の体制整備・拡充により、初期課題は徐々に解消し、専任教員による指導体制が確立するにつれ、満足度は向上してきたようである。
（エ）本専攻の特色である「イノベーション」の洗礼を受けたという印象は、修了生意識調査からはあまり強く感じられず、一般のビジネス・スクール卒業生の意識に近い評価とも言える。
（オ）修了生の本専攻への期待は強く、今後とも体制の一層の強化が必要である。特に
　・修了生の成功への継続的なサポート、修了生との多面的ネットワーク形成
　・本専攻の社会的な知名度、ブランド力向上、地域との一層の関係強化
　・本専攻の特色をより強く打ち出したプログラムの運営、グローバル化などの新しい環境への教育支援など
（カ）これらの調査結果は、いずれも貴重な材料なので、ぜひ今後の専攻の運営方針に生かしていくべきと考える。

5. 調査結果の詳細

（ア）調査対象
　表1が、2012年11月15日現在の専攻入学・修了状況数である。この内、調査時点（2012年7月）での修了生86名中、データベース上に連絡先が登録されている82名を本調査の対象とした。退学者・除籍者・現役在校生は対象外としている。

表1　イノベーションマネジメント専攻　入学者の修了状況（2012年11月15日現在）

入学年度	入学者（人）	修了者（人）	在学者（人）	退学者（人）	除籍者（人）	修了期間 規定年内	修了期間 規定年以上	修了率
※02	9	7	0	2	0	0	7	78%
03	19	16	0	2	1	4	12	84%
04	7	6	0	1	0	0	6	86%
05	17	10	0	6	1	7	3	59%
06	10	9	0	1	0	9	0	90%
07	17	13	0	3	1	7	6	76%
08	12	10	0	2	0	3	7	82%
09	12	10	1	1	0	7	3	82%
10	15	7	8	0	0	6	1	-
11	11	0	11	0	0	0	0	-
12	13	0	13	0	0	0	0	-
合計	142	88	33	18	3	43	45	-

※02年度修了者は（松本）からの編入生を含む

表2　調査票の配布、回収状況

入学年度	依頼修了者数	回答者数	回答率
02	7	3	43%
03	14	7	44%
04	6	4	67%
05	10	3	30%
06	7	1	11%
07	13	4	31%
08	10	7	70%
09	10	4	40%
10	5	3	60%
合計	82	36	44%

（イ）　調査表回収状況

調査表の配布と回収状況をまとめたのが、表2である。

全体の回収率は44％であった。記名・記述式のため　回答率は当初30％程度と見込んでいたので、予想以上に高かった。入学年度ごとに回答率のばらつきはあるが、10年間のプログラムの変遷を反映できる程度に各年代から万遍なく回答は得られていると考えている。

（ウ）　調査票の構成と主な質問項目

調査での質問項目と教育体験プロセスとの対応関係は、次頁の図の通りである。

基本的には、学生本人の「期待」とそれに対する本専攻の対応度、満足度などの主観的な評価認識を尋ねるものとなっている。全て記名、記述式である。なお調査票の写しを末尾に添付している。

（エ）　入学時の目的とその達成度（Q1，2）

表3は、修了生の入学時の期待目的と修了後の当初期待の達成度評価をまとめたものである。

これを見てわかるように、学生は幅広い目的意識をもって入学している。ミッドキャリアの学生は経営スキルの習得を重視している。経営者的な立場の学生は、経営に直結するものを期待している。また具体的な目的意識を持つ学生と、漠然とした「生き方探索」や「自分探し」の学生が併存している。一方、明示的に起業準備を目的とした者は、少ない。

こうした目的意識に対して、「修了後その目的を達成した」とする評価は全体で66％、約3分の2であった。

表4は、「入学時の期待目的が達せられなかった」とする評価の主な理由をまとめたものである。多様な理由が挙げられているが、やや重複してみられる理由としては、

・入学後に目的意識やテーマが変化したこと
・学んだことが生かせる場がないなどで、修了後に学びを実践できていないこと
・在学中により多く学べたのではないか、という悔悟
・期待に沿うプログラムがなかった　　など

があげられる。

総じて、修了生自身に起因する理由が主で、本専攻プログラムの不備に起因するものは多くはなさそうという印象である。

（オ）　入学前認識と入学後認識との合致・相違（Q3）

表5は、修了生が本専攻入学前に本専攻に抱いていた認識と、入学後の認識のギャップについて

●調査報告

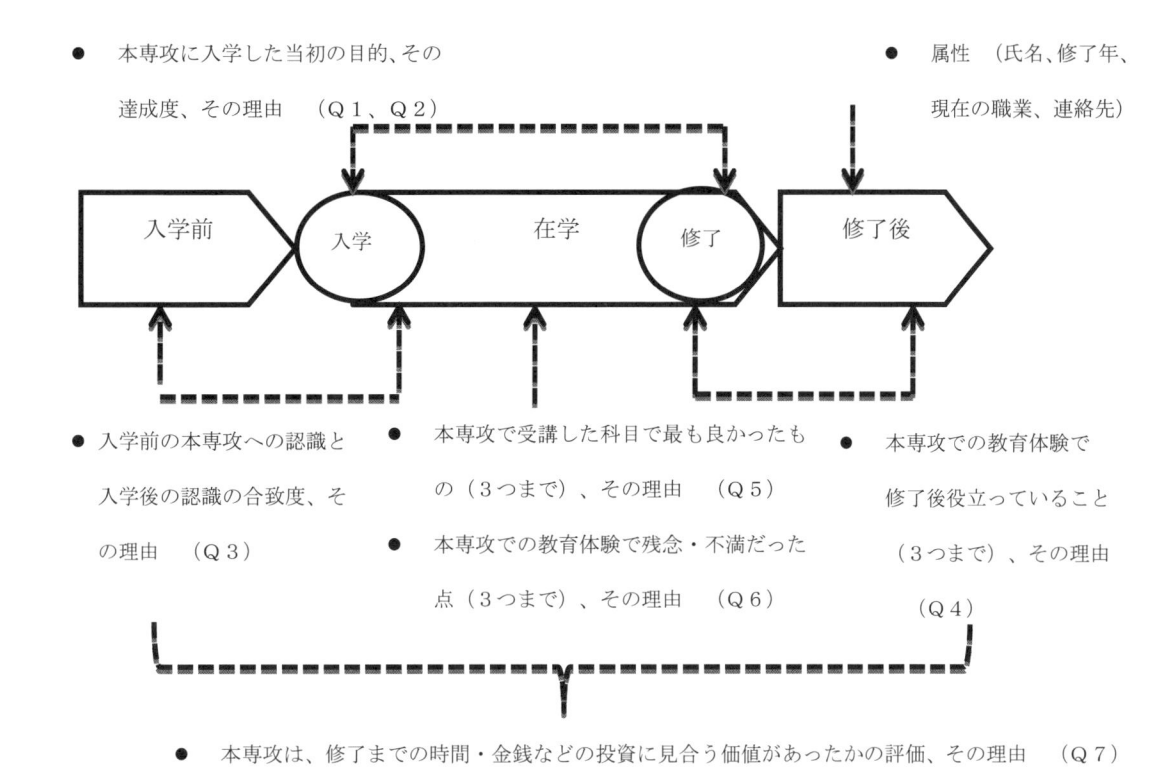

- 本専攻に入学した当初の目的、その達成度、その理由 （Q1、Q2）
- 属性（氏名、修了年、現在の職業、連絡先）

```
入学前 → 入学 → 在学 → 修了 → 修了後
```

- 入学前の本専攻への認識と入学後の認識の合致度、その理由（Q3）
- 本専攻で受講した科目で最も良かったもの（3つまで）、その理由（Q5）
- 本専攻での教育体験で残念・不満だった点（3つまで）、その理由（Q6）
- 本専攻での教育体験で修了後役立っていること（3つまで）、その理由（Q4）

- 本専攻は、修了までの時間・金銭などの投資に見合う価値があったかの評価、その理由（Q7）
- その他、感想・意見・提言を自由記入（Q8）

表3　入学の目的とその達成度評価（Q1、目的は複数回答あり）

入学時の目的	回答者	達成された (A)	されなかった (B)	どちらでもない (C)	わからない (D)	達成率 (A比率)
経営的なスキルアップ、経営知識習得	10	6	1	2	1	60%
自社・法人経営への活用（メーカー、小売、サービス、NPOなど）	9	6		1	2	67%
行政・学校マネジメントへの活用	5	4		1		80%
キャリアアップ／チェンジ、生き方変革	5	4	1			80%
人的ネットワーキング獲得	3	3				100%
会社指名・推薦時に目的を所与	2	1		1		50%
起業	2				2	0%
以下、特定知識・スキルを習得したい						
・企業の環境対策を学びたい	1	1				100%
・新製品プロジェクトの参考にしたい	1	1				100%
・新たなビジネスモデルを創りたい	1	1				100%
・サービス変革の参考にしたい	1	1				100%
・農業改革を学びたい	1	1				100%
・高齢者孤独死予防の参考にしたい	1	1				100%
・顧客の問題解決スキルを学びたい	1	1				100%
・組織改革の手法を学びたい	1			1		0%
・新製品開発手法を学びたい	1			1		0%
・IT活用と経営を学びたい	1			1		0%
・地域プロジェクトの参考にしたい	1			1		0%
全体	47	31	5	6	5	66%

表4　入学時の目標が「達成できた」と答えていない理由（Q2）

回答	年次	回答の理由
「達成されなかった」	03	・修論作成に意識と力を取られすぎて、目的だった組織改革手法の学習ができなかった
「達成されなかった」	04	・地域プロジェクトへの活用という目的から、子供のケアに焦点がシフト
「達成されなかった」	04	・経営知識の充電とネットワーキングは達成したが、経営と新しいITという目的は全く達成できなかった
「達成されなかった」	08	・農業起業目的だったが、初期投資が巨大となり断念。論文も書きたいことが書ききれず残念
「どちらでもない」	02	・自社の方向性の探索はできたが、経営の専門家をめざす目標はそもそも「奥深く」永遠に達成できない
「どちらでもない」	03	・日々の仕事に追われて、新製品の開発という目標に中なか結びつかない
「どちらでもない」	05	・民間の経営を行政に生かす目的は、学習はできたが、実践がともなわない
「どちらでもない」	06	・経営者の育成目的が、修了後の異動で不採算事業の立て直しになった
「どちらでもない」	07	・学習目的は達したが、もっと速く、多くを学ぶべきだった
「どちらでもない」	08	・NPO法人の経営方針は見いだせたが、「100年続く小売」という目標は、まだ未解決
「わからない」	05	・経営に関する知識・スキルを身に着けたい、という当初の目的は当たり前のことだった
「わからない」	10	・故郷に戻り起業するという目的だったが、まだ故郷に戻っていない

表5　入学前の認識と入学後の実際の違い（Q3）

	あまり違わない A	大きく違う B	どちらでもない C	わからない D	合計	合致比率（A比率）	相違比率（B比率）
02	1	1	1		3	33%	33%
03	2	4		1	7	29%	57%
04	2	1	1		4	50%	25%
05	2			1	3	67%	0%
06			1		1	0%	0%
07		1	3		4	0%	25%
08	3	4			7	43%	57%
09		1	2	1	4	0%	25%
10		3			3	0%	100%
合計	10	15	8	3	36	28%	42%

尋ねた結果である。

入学前と後との間に、多くの年代で、大きなギャップを感じた修了生が存在している。全体でも42％であるが、年代によっては、57〜100％である。逆に、「事前の認識通りだ」という修了生は、28％に過ぎない。

表6は、「入学前後の認識が大きく違う」と答えた人のその主な理由をまとめたものである。

「大きく違う」と答えた人の3分の2は、「期待よりも良かった」とポジティブなギャップとして認識している。特に、大学時代の教育とは大きく異なるプログラム内容、その実践性、教授方法、教員・同級生との交流などに強い印象を受けている。

一方、「期待外れ」と認識する人は、「かなり具体的・専門的な課題解決とそのための教育を期待したが獲得できなかった」、「もっと研究レベルが高いと思った」、あるいは「非実業系出身者への導入ケアが足りない」などを指摘している。

（カ）修了後役立っていること（Q4）

表7は、本専攻での教育体験で修了後役に立っていることを、主なもの3つまで挙げてもらった結果をまとめたものである。

修論作成や授業を通じて、思考法や課題解決方法が変わったことと、多様な人材との交流や人的ネットワーキングが、最も役立っていると認識されている。また特定課題研究で厳しい指導を受けたり、苦労して論文を完成させたりした経験が、達成感や成長、自信にもつながっているようである。

科目としては、経営・経済の基礎科目、マーケ

●調査報告

表6　入学前の認識と入学後の認識が大きく違うと答えた人の理由

年度		評価の方向
02	・期待以上のカリキュラムと講師陣、学生との交流が刺激になった	ポジティブ
03	・ビジネスマンを対象としており、それ以外の出身者への配慮に欠ける（経営学の予備知識などで）	ネガティブ
03	・行政の中だけでは習得できない思考方法をみにつけることができた	ポジティブ
03	・具体的な知識より課題に対する新たな視点の提示を受ける点が新鮮だった	ポジティブ
03	・新製品開発の具体的な手法を期待したが、経済の基礎的な内容が多かった	ネガティブ
04	・経営と新しい電子技術の結合を期待したが、専攻でも工学部でもカリキュラムはなかった	ネガティブ
07	・もっと敷居が高いと思ったが、それほどでもなかった	ポジティブ
08	・もっと研究レベルが高いと思っていた	ネガティブ
08	・学習する場所というより、目新しい世界だった。時流にも乗った感じがした。かけがいのない友達も得られた	ポジティブ
08	・教科書的な本の授業と応用・実技を分けて行うと思っていた	ポジティブ
08	・PC、ITを使わなくても商売が成り立つと思っていたが、すでに時代が変わっているのを痛感した	ポジティブ
09	・座学も実践的で、フィールドワークの講義もあった。県内企業の方々と知り合いになれた	ポジティブ
10	・高いレベルの講義、教員との親密なコミュニケーション、意見交換など学びも多く、視野も広がった	ポジティブ
10	・学生の延長かと思ったが、授業内容は学生の延長ではなかった	ポジティブ
10	・学生は中小企業の経営者と思ったが、多様な背景の学生がいた。詰め込み式の教育と思ったが、違った	ポジティブ

表7　本専攻での教育体験で修了後役に立っていること（主なもの3つまで）

項目	1番目	2番目	3番目	合計人数
思考法・問題へのアプローチ方法の学び（客観性、論理性、仮説思考など）	7	5	3	15
教員・同級生・修了生との交流、ネットワーク	3	8	4	15
特定課題研究の厳しい指導、論文の達成感	3	1	3	7
人間的な成長、自信、ガッツ	2	2	3	7
経営学の基礎知識、経済・経営用語	3	2	1	6
マーケティング、顧客志向	1	2	2	5
経営的な視野、経営者目線の獲得	4	0	0	4
ケーススタディ、成功失敗事例	2	2	0	4
企業の社会的責任、環境経営	1	1	2	4
経営戦略の基礎知識、企業ドメイン	1	2	0	3
継続学習・研究の場	0	0	3	3

ティング、ケーススタディ、CSR、経営戦略などの役立ち感が強い。また終了後、本専攻を継続学習・研究の場として、認識する修了生も一部存在している。

（キ）　受講して良かった科目（Q5）
表8は、本専攻で受講してよかったと認識している科目を3つまで挙げてもらった結果をまとめたものである。★印を付した科目は、当時の非常勤教員が講じたものである。
初期は、経営戦略論、経営組織論などの基本科目に加えて、工学系の科目、専門性の高い科目に対する評価が高い。また体制整備途上でもあったためか、外部講師の開講科目への評価も高い。
近年になると、マーケティングやロジカルプレゼンテーションなどへの好評価が加わる一方、外部講師や工学系科目のウェイトは相対的に減少している。
本専攻の看板である「イノベーション概論」「プロジェクト演習」「特定課題研究指導」「グリーンMOT科目」などへの評価がさほどでもないのが、気になる点である。

表8　受講してよかった科目（3つまで）カッコ内はそれぞれ挙げた人数

	1番目に挙げた科目・教員	2番目に挙げた科目・教員	3番目に挙げた科目・教員
02 （2名）	経営組織論（柴田）（2）	経営戦略論（鈴木・茂木）（1） 会計（星野）★（1）	特許戦略論（生越）★（1） 組織の診断と革新（今村）★（1）
03 （6名）	経営戦略論（鈴木・茂木）（2） 経営組織論（柴田）（1） 特定課題研究（茂木）（1） 規制緩和と経営政策（柴田）（1） グローバル化・・・（樋口）（1） 組織の診断と革新（今村）★（1）	技術開発論（山沢）（2） 特許戦略論（生越）★（1） 精密機械工学特論（松岡）（1） フードマーケティング（茂木）（1） 組織の診断と革新（今村）★（1）	行政組織と政策過程（沼尾）（1） 証券化とポートフォリオ（上地）（1） 事業化戦略と金融新潮流（真壁）（1） フードマーケティング（茂木）（1） 技術開発と事業化（赤羽）★（1） 外部講師特別講義★（1）
04 （3名）	経営戦略論（鈴木）（1） 技術開発論（山沢）（1） 技術開発と事業化（赤羽）★（1）	経営戦略論（鈴木）（1） 組織の診断と革新（今村）★（1）	 特許戦略論（生越）★（1） 組織の診断と革新（今村）★（1）
05 （3名）	経営組織論（柴田）（1） 特定課題研究（樋口）（1） 特定課題研究（柴田）（1）	組織論特論（柴田）（1） プロジェクト演習（1） 組織の診断と革新（今村）★（1）	マーケティング論（茂木）（1） 技術開発と事業化（赤羽）★（1）
06			
07 （4名）	マーケティング論（牧田）（1） ロジカルプレゼン（牧田）（1） 経営戦略論（鈴木）（1） 組織の診断と革新（今村）★（1）	マーケティング論（牧田）（1） ロジカルシンキング（牧田）（1） 経営戦略論（鈴木）（1） プロジェクト演習（1）	企業の社会的責任（樋口）（1） 経営組織論（柴田）（1） 技術開発と事業化（赤羽）★（1） イノベーション概論（特に客員）★
08 （6名）	経営組織論（柴田）（3） 経営戦略論（鈴木）（2） プロジェクト演習（柴田）（1） プロジェクト演習（牧田）（1）	マーケティング論（牧田）（4） 知的財産戦略（加藤）★（1） 組織の診断と革新（今村）★（1）	ロジカルプレゼン（牧田）（1） プロジェクト演習（鈴木）（1） プロジェクト演習（柴田）（1） 組織の診断と革新（今村）★（1）
09 （3名）	ロジカルプレゼン（牧田）（1） 企業の社会的責任（樋口）（1） 特定課題研究（柴田）（1）	ロジカルプレゼン（牧田）（1） マーケティング論（牧田）（1） 市場関連特論（樋口）（1） 組織の診断と革新（今村）★（1）	ロジカルプレゼン（牧田）（1） サステナビリティ概論（ノートン） 経営組織論（柴田）（1）
10 （3名）	マーケティング論（牧田）（1） 特定課題研究（牧田）（1） 経営戦略論（鈴木）（1）	応用マーケティング論（牧田）（1） ロジカルプレゼン（牧田）（2）	企業の社会的責任（樋口）（1） プロジェクト演習（柴田）（1） 組織の診断と革新（今村）（1）

注：★は非常勤教員

（ク）　残念・不満だったこと（Q3）

表9は、本専攻で残念だった点、不満を感じた点で比較的回答の多かったものをまとめたものである。

働きながら学ぶ社会人学生が多いため、開講時間・時期の問題指摘が最も多い。特に、夕方18時の開講時間に対する不満が強い。

専攻開設初期の体制不備への不満も強い。その指摘の多くは、現在はかなり改善されているが、学生に不自由を感じさせた点があったことは率直に反省する必要がある。教育内容・質、プログラム・教員の体制、サポート体制などへの課題指摘は、現在改善されているものもあるが、依然課題となっている部分も少なくない。

（ケ）　本専攻への時間・金銭投資と教育価値は見合っているか（Q7）

表10は、専攻での教育に対する時間的・金銭的な投資に見合う教育体験だったかを尋ねた問いへの回答状況である。

全体で72％の修了生が、投下した時間・金銭に見合う教育価値を見出している。見合っていないと答えた修了生は、6％（2名）に過ぎない。

表11は、ここでの時間・金銭投資の価値判断の主な理由をまとめたものである。

「見合う」と判断した人は、人脈や多様な人たちとの交流、自らの成長、コスト・パフォーマンスの良さ、プログラムの中身の濃さなどに投資価値を見出している。Q4での「修了後に役立っていること」に関する回答結果と響き合う印象である。

一方、「見合わない」と判断した理由は、学費

表9　本専攻で残念だった点、不満を感じた点（回答の.比較的多かったもの）

回答数	主なテーマ	主なコメント例
11	開講時間・時期に関する不満	・平日授業開始が18：00では社会人は通いにくい ・週末開講を増やすなど、受講時間のフレキシビリティを高めてほしい ・合同研究指導の時期、ジョイント・ディグリー学生の論文の提出時期の見直し
10	本専攻開講初期の問題への不満	・プログラムの未整備 ・教員のレベル・認識のバラツキ ・施設・設備の不備、情報提供・説明不足（グリーンＭＯＴ学生への対応含む）
9	教育内容・質への不満	・グループスタディの少なさ ・会計系プログラムのレベルへの不満 ・技術系・理系科目の数・レベルへの不満 ・一部教員の教授法・質への不満 ・より実務的・問題解決型にしてもらいたい
8	プログラム・教員の欠如への不満	・ＩＴ経営やスポーツマネジメントなど学びたいプログラムの欠如 ・海外視察の断絶、欠如 ・他学部・他校との交流・単位互換の不足、欠如
8	学生サポート体制の不備への不満	・秋入学学生へのサポート、説明不足 ・女子学生へのケア不足（男性中心の印象） ・修了後キャリアへのサポート不足・学生数の少なさ、交流の浅さ（修了後も含め）
7	自分自身への不満・反省	・特定課題研究の掘り下げ不足、検証不足、テーマの拡散 ・学習・交流時間の不足、努力不足

表10　専攻への時間・金銭投資に見合う教育だったか（Ｑ７）

	見合っている A	見合っていない B	わからない C	その他 D	合計	見合っている （A比率）	見合っていない （B比率）
02	3				3	100%	0 %
03	5	2			7	71%	29%
04	3			1	4	75%	0 %
05	1		1	1	3	33%	0 %
06			1		1	0 %	0 %
07	3		1		4	75%	0 %
08	7				7	100%	0 %
09	1		1	2	4	25%	0 %
10	3				3	100%	0 %
合計	26	2	4	4	36	72%	6 %

負担の重さ、一部教育内容の問題点（開設初期）などによる。「分からない」他の判断は、学習成果が実践できておらず時期尚早という理由による。また、工学部博士課程とのジョイント・ディグリーの学生は、本専攻への「追加投資」負担感が希薄ということのようである。

（コ）　感想・意見・提言（Q8）

表12は、本専攻への感想、意見、提言などを内容別のまとめたものである。

多数のコメントを頂いている。本専攻だけではなく、同窓会運営など修了後の支援や継続学習などへの期待や要望を多数含まれている。

謝辞

最後になるが、ご多忙中にも関わらず、記名・記述式の面倒くさいアンケートに快くご協力を賜りました修了生の皆様に、本専攻の教職員一同を代表して、深く感謝申し上げたい。

(2012年12月18日投稿、12月27日受理)

付録資料

調査票　写し

表11　投資価値の主な判断理由

投資価値への見合い判断の主な理由	人数
「投資に見合う」と答えた理由	
人脈・出会い、異業種・経営者との交流があった	10
自分の成長、自信、価値観・視野の拡大	7
コスト・パフォーマンスが高い、4年いられたこと	6
中味の濃い授業、高い講師のレベル、少人数	6
論文完遂の喜び、達成感	3
継続学習の習慣、相談の場	2
「投資に見合わない」と答えた理由	
主婦・家族持ちには学費負担が重い	2
学費に見合わないつまらない授業もあった	1
使える人的ネットワークが不十分	1
入学目的が未達に終わった	1
「分からない」・「その他」と答えた理由	
まだ実践で成果が出ていない	3
博士課程とジョイントで追加学費はゼロ	2
いくら払ったか覚えていない	1

表12　本専攻への感想、意見、提言などの自由記述

主な内容	年次	感想・意見・提言
プログラム内容・質への提言	03	大学としての講義ができる講師か精査してほしい。
	03	授業評価でマイナスを受けた講義の見直しをしてほしい。
	03	どれくらいニーズがあるか不明だが、研究を展開・深化させるための博士課程の開講。
	04	経営に関係する電子技術関連科目の開講、議論の場の設営
	04	外部講師の招聘の継続、拡大
	04	県内の行政・経済界などへの学校もコミット拡大、修了生も交えて県内貢献の機会を増大
	04	海外への視察機会の拡大
	04	工学部他信大各学部との交流拡大、人的ネットワーク拡大して、産学協同を広げる
	04	他の経営大学院との交流拡大、論文発表会への参加など
	04	公開講座が少なくなった。あれば会社の中堅を誘える
	05	全国的な経営に加えて県内企業経営者との懇談、県内企業を意識したカリキュラムも充実してほしい
	07	現役経営者・修了生を交えたグループ討議がもっとできればよい。ケースではないリアルな経営の声、事例を聞きたい。

本専攻体験の感想、本専攻への感謝、声援	08	入口は低くても出口は厳しくしたほうが本人のためでもある
	03	大学院での苦労を思えば、現在の仕事の困難は何とかなるという自信がついた
	03	新しい観点でビジネスを見ることができ、人生の大きな財産となった。特にPLC上の自社製品の位置づけなど。長い付き合いを期待。
	07	教員・学生・職員に感謝。貴重な経験
	02	今後のさらなる活躍を期待
	04	教員・出会いに感謝
	04	自己変革の機会になったことを感謝
	08	在学中は厳しく、折れそうになった。修了できて自分を褒めている
	08	これからよい伝統が築かれることを願う
	08	とことん生徒を追い込む授業はいつまでも心に残る。追い込まれた時の反応を見守ってほしい
	08	多くの出会いは新鮮で有意義だった
	09	貴重な体験。修了生が増えると現役とのバランスがやや心配。
	10	当初の目標は未達だが、指導を受けて新たな目標が生まれた。頑張りたい。入学してお得だった。感謝。
修了後の継続学習や同窓会運営への期待・提言・要望	02	修了生にも参加できる講義・プロジェクト演習(例：柴田・今村両教員)を今後も継続してほしい。
	03	修了生の参加できるイベントの増加。教員・各界との交流、共同アウトプット、地域企業団体との交流、学校・現役・OBの一体企画など。
	03	今年度から始まった修了生にも参加できる講義の充実を期待。できれば外部講師は、修了生も受講しやすい週末開講を希望。
	04	学校を軸にした修了生の交流拡大。同窓会の役割が重要。
	05	同窓会以外で長く専攻と関われる仕組み(修了後も指導を受けられる、共同で研究できる、地域に貢献できるなど)
	07	同窓会の活躍・情報発信を期待
	07	修了すると学校に行く機会は少ない。博士課程をつくってほしい。
	09	修了後もOB公開講座(プロジェクト演習)、同窓会、SGCなどで大学との繋がりを感じ、感謝。
	03	専攻の知名度の低さ。もっとPRしてほしい。修了生にも募集要項などを送って、学生募集のサポートを受けるべき
本専攻の知名度向上への期待・提言	10	知名度の向上、同窓会のつながりの強化を期待。経営大学院の存在自体を知らない経営者が数多い。PR方法の工夫を期待。
	10	同窓会の会費徴収方法を見直してほしい。サラリーマンには、数万円の出費は厳しい。

信州大学 大学院イノベーション・マネジメント専攻（経営大学院）での
教育体験に関するフィードバック　　　アンケート調査　記入用紙

あなたご自身について教えてください

お名前　＿＿＿＿＿＿＿＿＿＿＿＿＿＿＿　メール アドレス　＿＿＿＿＿＿＿＿＿＿＿＿＿＿＿

大学院修了年　＿＿＿＿＿＿＿＿＿＿＿＿＿　電話　＿＿＿＿＿＿＿＿＿＿＿＿＿＿＿

現在のご職業　＿＿＿＿＿＿＿＿＿＿＿＿＿＿＿＿＿＿＿＿＿＿＿＿＿＿＿＿＿＿＿＿＿＿＿

Q1. そもそも、あなたご自身が経営大学院に入学された当初の目的は何でしたか？

＿＿＿

＿＿＿

Q2. その当初の目的は達成されましたか？　（一つお選び下さい）

　　　☐ 達成された　　☐ 達成されなかった　　☐ どちらでもない　　☐ わからない

「達成された」とご評価される方は、どのように達成されましたか？

＿＿＿

＿＿＿

それ以外のご評価の方は、なぜそのようにご評価されますか？

＿＿＿

＿＿＿

Q3. あなたが、経営大学院に対してご入学前に持たれていたご認識と、ご入学後のご認識は大きく違っていたでしょうか？　（一つお選び下さい）

　　　☐ あまり違わなかった　　☐ 大きく違っていた　　☐ どちらでもない　　☐ わからない

「違っていた」とお答えの方は、どのように違っていたのか、お教えください。

＿＿＿

●調査報告

Q4. あなたの経営大学院での教育体験の中で、修了後もっとも役に立っていることを最大3つまで上げてください。またどのように役に立っているか、についても教えてください。

修了後、もっとも役立っていること（1）
_____

その理由
_____

修了後、もっとも役立っていること（2）
_____

その理由
_____

修了後、もっとも役立っていること（3）
_____

その理由
_____

Q5. あなたが経営大学院で受けた科目の中で、もっとも良かった科目を3つまで挙げてください。またその理由も教えてください。

もっとも良かった科目（1）
_____

その理由
_____

もっとも良かった科目（2）
_____

その理由
_____

もっとも良かった科目（3）
_____

その理由
_____

Q6. あなたの経営大学院での教育体験の中で、残念だった点・不満だった点があれば、3つまで挙げてください。またその理由も教えてください。

残念だった点・不満だった点（1）

その理由

残念だった点・不満だった点（2）

その理由

残念だった点・不満だった点（3）

その理由

Q7. あなたは、経営大学院に 2 年＋αの時間と授業料＋αの費用を投資されたわけですが、経営大学院での教育は、それに見合う価値があったとお考えですか？　（一つお選びください）

☐ 十分見合っている　　☐ 見合っていない　　☐ わからない　　☐ その他

なぜそのようにご評価されるのか、理由をお聞かせ下さい。

Q8. この他に、ご感想・ご意見があれば、ぜひご自由にご記入ください。また今後の経営大学院の教育に関して、ご意見やご提言があれば、ぜひお願い致します。

ご協力ありがとうございました！

『イノベーション・マネジメント研究』
"Journal of Innovation Management"
投稿規程

　信州大学大学院　イノベーション・マネジメント専攻は、大学と社会との交流を積極的に推進し、産官学の連携を企て、技術知識とマネジメント手法を修得した有能な人材を社会に輩出することを目的として、設立されました。本誌『イノベーション・マネジメント研究』も、この専攻目的に沿って、編集・刊行してまいります。

　従いまして、従来の大学紀要などのように学術論文に限定して記事を収集したり、また、多くの学会誌に見られるように、執筆者を学会員に限定したりすることは、本誌の編集意図とするところではありません。

　学術論文に留まらずに、調査報告や事例研究、実験報告、企画提案など広くイノベーションに関連する創造性のあるものを収集して、これらを産業と社会のイノベーションに関心を寄せる方々に提供してまいりたいと存じます。そのために、学界だけでなく実業界で活動する実務家を含めて、広範囲からの投稿を歓迎いたします。

　しかしながら、本誌の刊行目的を担保しつつ掲載原稿の質を確保することに腐心しなくてはならないことはいうまでもありません。そこで、投稿原稿は、全て本誌編集委員会による審査を受けることとし、所定の水準を満たしたものを掲載することといたします。

1．投稿者
　　本専攻科の設立趣旨に賛同するものであれば、資格要件を問わずに誰でも投稿できる。
2．原稿言語
　　和文または英文とする。その他の言語を希望するものは、事前に編集委員会まで申し出て、了解をうることとする。英文原稿は、和文タイトルと和文要旨を添付する。
3．原稿の掲載
　　投稿原稿のうち論文は、編集委員会が定めるところにより専門家・識者による査読を経て、編集委員会が掲載の採択を決定する。その他の投稿原稿は、編集委員会による協議を経て、掲載を決定する。編集委員会は、本誌が掲載する予定の原稿全てについて、原稿の内容や形式について著者に説明または修正を要求できるものとし、また、編集作業上の観点から校閲する権限を有する。
4．原稿の執筆要領
　　原稿の執筆要領の詳細は、「『イノベーション・マネジメント研究』投稿細則」による。
5．原稿の受理
　　原稿の受理日は、編集委員会が原稿の掲載を承認した日とする。
6．原稿の著作権利
　　本誌に掲載された著作物の著作権は著者に帰属し、本誌は編集著作権を有するものとする。著者は、これの著作権の行使を本編集委員会に委託するものとするが、当該著作者が自らこれを行使することもできる。

附則　2004年6月30日よりこれを施行する。

『イノベーション・マネジメント研究』
投稿細則

　『イノベーション・マネジメント研究』への投稿原稿は、以下に示す規程に準拠して執筆するものとする。

1．原稿分量は、図表を含め400字詰原稿用紙（換算）50枚以内を目安とする。これを超えるものについては、あらかじめ編集委員会の承認を得るものとする。
2．投稿原稿の様式は、ワープロA4用紙（縦置き横書き）に横書き、新仮名遣いを原則とする。図表は、適切な大きさに縮小して、原稿とは別のA4用紙に1点ずつ描きまたは貼付し、それぞれ一連番号をつけて、可能な限り完全版下状態にて提出する。但し、図表の体裁が簡潔で、ワープロ原稿に挿入して差し支えないものなどについては、別用紙への貼付方法に依らなくともよいものとする。
3．投稿原稿の章立て、注記、引用文献などの扱いは、学術論文の作法に準じ、引用などに当たって許諾の必要なものは、執筆者の責任において、投稿前にあらかじめ権利者からの承諾を得ておくこととする。
4．投稿原稿は、本原稿をA4用紙にコピーしたもの4部を、所定の「投稿論文など審査申込書」を添えて編集委員会宛に提出する。投稿者は、必ず元原稿を手元に用意して、編集委員会からの問い合わせや再提出の要請に即応できるようにしておくこととする。なお、編集委員会からの要請以外の理由による原稿提出後の訂正などには応ずることはできない。
5．投稿原稿のテーマや内容、形式によっては、所定の審査料を請求する場合がある。
6．審査を通過した論文などの投稿者は、編集委員会の求めに応じてDOSのテキストファイルに収録したフロッピーを編集委員会あてに提出することを原則とし、これに準じたかたちで提出することも可とする。図表についても、本誌製版作成技術上の規格に合わせた電子編集可能な媒体にて提出することが望ましい。編集委員会の求めるところ以外の仕様による場合は、入力作業費及び版下作成費を投稿者に求めるものとする。
7．著者校正は原則として1回とするが、編集委員会の認める事由がある場合には追加することができる。校正に要する時間は編集委員会の指示による。
8．原稿の抜き刷りは作成しないが、希望のあるものについては実費相当分を負担して作成することができる。
9．投稿者は、掲載誌を2部提供される。共同執筆者についても同様とする。それ以上の要求がある場合には、編集委員会に申し出て協議する。
10．投稿宛て先は、信州大学大学院イノベーション・マネジメント専攻内『イノベーション・マネジメント研究』編集委員会宛とする。投稿締切日は特に設けず、常時受け付ける。

附則　2004年6月30日よりこれを施行する。

『イノベーション・マネジメント研究』
編集委員会細則

1．イノベーション・マネジメント専攻は、専攻誌『イノベーション・マネジメント研究』を編集・刊行することを目的として、編集委員会を置く。
2．編集委員会は、編集委員長1名と編集委員若干名により構成される。
3．編集委員長は、専攻会議にて専任教官の中から選出されたものとする。編集委員は、編集委員長の指名を受けたものとし、編集委員長と編集委員の総数の半数以下であれば、同専攻教官以外の編集委員を任命できるものとする。
4．編集委員会は、本誌の編集全体を所管する。編集委員会は、投稿原稿などを審査し、査読を対象とするものと、それ以外のものに仕分けする。
5．査読対象論文は、編集委員会が査読員を2名選出して、査読を依頼する。
6．査読員は、査読結果を所定の査読報告書により、編集委員会に報告する。編集委員会は、査読の結果に基づいて掲載の可否を決定する。査読員2名の見解が著しくかけ離れるときには、編集委員会が総合的に判断して、掲載の可否を決定する。この場合、査読員を追加して、判断材料を追加することを妨げない。
7．査読員の氏名は、原則として公表しない。
8．査読のために、試験研究・調査の実施、新規文献の購入、遠方の外部査読員との協議など、特別の経費が発生する場合には、所定の範囲内で、論文投稿者に査読審査料を請求することができるものとする。
9．編集委員会は、査読対象論文以外の原稿の掲載の可否を決定する。また、必要に応じて、これらを校閲する。
10．編集委員会は、原稿執筆者に掲載の採択の可否について通知する。その際に、原稿の修正を要求することができるものとする。また、タイトルならびに英文タイトルについて助言できるものとする。
11．編集委員長の任期は、専攻会議にて決める。編集委員の任期は、編集長が指名してこれを受諾した日から、解任の通知を受理した日までとする。但し、専攻会議にて決定がある場合には、それに従うものとする。

附則　2004年6月30日よりこれを施行する。

イノベーション・マネジメント研究 【第8号】

2013年3月21日発行

編　　　者：信州大学 経営大学院　編集委員会
　　　　　　〒380-8553　長野県長野市若里 4-17-1
　　　　　　TEL 026-269-5696／FAX 026-269-5699
　　　　　　http://www.im.shinshu-u.ac.jp/

発　行　者：筑紫　恒男

発　行　所：(株)建帛社
　　　　　　〒112-0011　東京都文京区千石 4-2-15
　　　　　　〔営業部〕TEL 03-3944-2611／FAX 03-3946-4377
　　　　　　http://www.kenpakusha.co.jp/

定価1,000円
（本体952円＋税5％）

©信州大学 経営大学院 2013　　　　　　DTP／印刷・製本：亜細亜印刷株式会社